network or perish

learn the secrets of master networkers

robyn henderson

belinda yabsley

neen james

kim m^c guinness

jennifer jefferies

lee-anne carson

sue henry

sandy forster

✦ what's in this book? ✦

robyn henderson – Not only is networking an essential life skill, but also the most basic business building tool in today's competitive market. Robyn is a Global Networking Specialist and shares the secrets of master networkers, tips on how to make a great first impression, insights into new millennium networking – and solves the problem of how to turn networking activity into an endless stream of referrals.

belinda yabsley – Find out the networking secrets that have made Belinda the most successful new luxury vehicle sales consultant in Australia, and how the life-lessons her parents taught her can help anyone to improve their business.

neen james – Make the most of your time and energy with Neen's productivity-based approach to networking. Find out how to identify the best networking opportunities, make the most of the time you spend networking and how to engage and connect with people. Neen also explains how you can create your own network and how she uses networking as a key marketing strategy in her own successful business.

sue henry – Good networking is simply a matter of good habits. Sue explains the essentials of a simple networking system that will suit you and help you to leverage your business through strong networking habits.

jennifer jefferies – One of the best-kept secrets of successful networking ever! Jennifer shows you how you can overcome your anxieties and create a powerful, positive and lasting impression at every networking event by tapping into the potent properties of nature's own essential oils.

lee-anne carson – Lee-Anne's one-year-old son has a networking lesson from the sandbox for all of us! Find out how to get back in touch with your inner networking instincts, and discover how to position yourself in the 'inner circle' with Lee-Anne's ten secrets to making and cultivating influential connections.

kim mcguinness – If you're spending too much time working in your business (or career) and not enough time working on your business (or career), you need a networking strategy. Kim explains why a deliberate approach to networking should be a key element in your strategic plan. Founder of the enormously successful Businesswomen's Breakfast Series, Kim also offers some valuable insight into how to seek and manage relationships with sponsors

sandy forster – Great news for all non-networkers, Sandy has discovered the easy way to network and become Wildly Wealthy in the process! Find out how Sandy grew a $2,000,000 business in just five months through networking and creating strategic alliances.

© Copyright Robyn Henderson 2004

All rights reserved. No part of this publication may be reproduced, stored in a retrieval system, or transmitted in any form or by any means, electronic, mechanical, photocopying, recording or otherwise, without the written permission of the publisher.

Cover Design: Karen Curran, Unicorn Graphics www.unicorngraphics.com.au

Typesetting: Toni Esser, Living Energy email: toni@livingenergy.com.au

Editing: Simone Tregeagle, email: simone@inkcommunications.com.au

Printed in Australia by Watson, Ferguson & Co. Qld.

ISBN: 0-9752494-2-8

Henderson, Robyn; Yabsley, Belinda; James, Neen; Henry, Sue; McGuinness, Kim; Jefferies, Jennifer; Carson, Lee-Anne; Forster, Sandy.

Network or Perish

Includes index

1. Business building skills. 2. Communication in management.
2. People networking

Sea Change Publishing
PO Box 1596,
Kingscliff NSW 2487 Australia
www.seachangepublishing.com.au
info@seachangepublishing.com.au

✦ table of contents ✦

✦ introduction ✦

Networking has become a vital component of the business and personal marketing mix – yet few people truly maximise their daily networking opportunities. Many people still see networking as something they do, rather than something they live. Wise networkers incorporate the basic universal laws of reciprocity, abundance and giving without expectation as a foundation of beliefs and values in their lives.

And more and more as unethical behaviour or practices are revealed on a local, national and international basis, there is a growing need for people to do business with people that they know like and trust. Network or perish may sound like a strong statement – yet it is true, if you are not networking, there is a strong chance your business and career will not thrive and may even perish.

Are master networkers born or made? I believe networking is a learned skill and everyone (without exception) can improve their networking skills by observing and copying the habits of those who network well.

In bringing the book Network or Perish together, I looked at my own networks filled with many spheres of influence and key players from all walks of life. The criteria for contributors for this book was firstly identifying a number of key influences, who had strong reputations in their respective fields, were known to be givers rather than takers, were good communicators and most importantly were prepared to share their stories in print.

Each author shares their "secrets", habits, ideas, strategies and instinctive networking practices that have enabled each of them to build successful businesses, networks and careers, whilst building a reputation for being a master networker.

A word of advice, read this book with two different coloured highlight pens close by. And as you read the many ideas, tips and systems discussed throughout the book, highlight those tips you need to implement immediately with one colour highlight pen and those ideas that you may choose to implement within the next six months with the second colour highlight pen. This will make re-reading the book an easier task and you will have an instant networking action plan as you finish reading the book.

I encourage you to fine tune your networking skills every week by trying at least one different idea from this comprehensive book – they say that practice makes perfect and the more you network, the easier networking will be come for you. I also recommend that you share this book with your own network and visit the various author's websites for even more ideas, articles and ebooks.

Always remember that networking can open any door in the world for you and that the window of opportunity is so clear, that sometimes we miss it.

Happy networking

Robyn Henderson

chapter one

the secrets of master networkers

robyn henderson

Master networkers know that networking is a life skill, not just something that they do in the hope of being rewarded; they live and lead by embracing the basic philosophy of treating people in the same way that they would like to be treated and understand that the practice of networking is ruled by three immutable universal laws:

Abundance. Master networkers do not fear competition because they believe there are abundant opportunities for everyone.

Reciprocity. Master networkers understand that what you give out comes back to you tenfold – when you give out positivity, you will receive positivity; when you give out referrals, you will receive referrals; and when you give out negativity, you will receive negativity.

Giving without expectation. Master networkers give without remembering and receive without forgetting. They do things for other people, not in the hope of receiving anything in return, but simply to help someone else achieve their goals.

As you read through this book you will share in the lessons and networking techniques of some of Australia's true master networkers. You will learn why networking is a vital component of your business or personal marketing mix, how you can achieve more through effective networking than through just about any other promotional or marketing activity, how you can develop your own networking plans and style and find out how some people have put networking to work with extraordinary success. You will understand how you can tap into the benefits of networking and why the following fundamental principles and practices of networking must become part of your life-skill set.

Cross-networking with competitors. Master networkers form strategic alliances with their competitors. They don't see competition, rather they see opportunities for everyone – and they know that often these will come through competitive alliances.

Calling people names. Master networkers know that calling someone by their name is one of the greatest compliments that you can give. One well-known Australian airline CEO was on a first name basis with everyone from the cargo porter to the kitchen hand. No matter where he went throughout the tarmac or terminal he greeted people by their first name and won the respect of everyone. During his time as CEO industrial disputes were unheard of.

More networking = less advertising. Master networkers know that the more they network through well-chosen functions and events, the less they need to advertise.

Income building versus income generating. Income generating is at the core of every business. It is how the business makes money in the short term and is a critical task. Income building is about networking, following up, keeping in touch, showing that you care, giving referrals and maintaining contacts. It is neither critical nor urgent and is often left to chance; however, it is a very important task. Master networkers invest time in networking every day and know that it is critical to the future of their business.

Everyone is a sphere of influence. Master networkers ensure that everyone in their organisation has a professional business card and is encouraged to use it. No one is considered a nobody – everyone is a sphere of influence somewhere in society.

Building business by building business. Revenue enhancement is about making money for your clients. Whether it is done by introducing one client to another at a meeting or event or referring one client to another when asked for a recommendation, revenue enhancement is one of the fastest ways to create loyalty; you are earning the right to do business again and again and tapping into the law of reciprocity – what you give out is what you get back. When you start giving away referrals, you start receiving them, and not necessarily from the same place you gave them.

Avoiding complacency. Master networkers know that avoiding complacency is critical in today's competitive marketplace. Sometimes we can fall into the trap of taking clients for granted. We stop returning calls within 24 hours, acknowledging emails and solving small problems as they occur. But when small problems are not dealt with, they become big problems and unresolved problems become lost advocates. Master networkers know that they cannot afford to lose advocates.

Cultivating broad networks. Master networkers avoid falling into the trap of only networking within their own industry or profession. They network across a board age, industry and geographical spectrum. The easiest way to keep abreast of what is happening in your industry, city and community is to network across a number of sectors. Master networkers cultivate a variety of contacts and know who to connect with to find the answer to most problems. People seek out master networkers as spheres of influence – and know that if they don't know the answer, they will know someone who does.

Making connections from the heart. Master networkers make heart-to-heart connections – they are present in the moment and listen with their hearts as well as their ears. When you speak with them you know that they are with you and not distracted or thinking about something else. As a result you feel comfortable because you know you are being listened to every time.

chapter two

a strategic approach to networking

kim mcguiness

What is a networking strategy? Why do you need one? Is networking really that important?

Consider these two scenarios:

Sally has just started her own business. She is convinced that she is too busy to network, even though she knows how beneficial it could be. She spends her time working in the business, not on the business – an age-old problem – and networking gets pushed to the bottom of her 'to do' list.

She finally makes time to go along to the local Chamber of Commerce function – just to show her face. She arrives late and flustered, in time to hear the speaker being introduced, and sits at the back of the room. After the event, aware that she only has a limited amount of time to network, she races around introducing herself to as many people as possible. The next day she spends a demoralising session cold-calling potential clients; and she never again hears from any of the people she met the previous evening.

Oli*via manages a department within a large company and is well aware that networking has been critical to her success. She has been attending two networking events regularly and knows the hosts of each quite well. She chose her networking groups carefully, researching the events and the calibre of people who attend them.*

One morning she arrived at a breakfast event early and met Jenny, a 'first-timer', over coffee as guests were registering. The two women spent quality time getting to know each other: Olivia learnt that Jenny had recently started her own executive coaching company and although she had no use for a coach (her company offers a coaching and mentoring program) she listened with great interest to Jenny's story and took Jenny under her wing for the duration of the event. Olivia introduced herself and Jenny to the guests at her table and initiated a discussion on a news article she had read the previous day.

At the end of the event, the host introduced another person, Karen, to Olivia. Karen had been attending for a while and the host had just learnt that Karen was in a complementary industry to Olivia and thought the two should meet. Olivia, Karen and Jenny had a great chat over coffee in a nearby café after the breakfast and agreed to meet up again at the next month's event.

The following day, Olivia received a call from Jenny to thank her for making the event so comfortable and enjoyable. Jenny mentioned that she had been speaking to a number of people about the great time she had at the breakfast and that many of them were interested in coming along to the next one. Olivia told Jenny that while she was speaking to her husband about the new friend she met at the breakfast, she discovered that his company is looking for a coach to head up a training program and asked whether Jenny would be interested in pitching for the business.

The following month, Olivia, Karen and Jenny met at the breakfast along with Jenny's four new guests. Over time, Karen and Olivia became alliance partners and grew each other's businesses substantially. Jenny became an advocate for Olivia's business and referred numerous potential clients.

Jenny, Karen and Olivia continue to meet many new people at the breakfast events; business referrals bounce around between the three women and their contacts – and their contact's contacts – on a regular basis. Olivia has not had the need to cold call a client in months.

Which scenario would you prefer?

Networking is everywhere; it is the people you meet every day – and it's no secret that it is a valuable tool that can help you develop your business and your career.

So what is a networking strategy and why do you need one? Why do you need to actively network – surely the people you meet in your daily dealings are enough? For some that may be the case…but have you ever heard about someone coming across a brilliant job or business opportunity through some obscure connection? Have you ever bumped into someone you haven't had contact with for years, only to find that there is incredible synergy between the two of you at that point in time? It does happen – and networking is a valuable investment in making sure that you are in the right place at the right time to make these connections, rather than just hoping that the people in your every day will be enough.

A networking strategy is about making the most of your time and the networking opportunities available to you. These days everyone is busy, pressed for time, and active networking gets pushed to the bottom of the 'to do' list in favour of more 'urgent' activities – it's the classic problem of working in your business (or career), rather than on your business (or career). Instead of pushing networking to the bottom of the priority list why not make it an important part of your business or career development plan and devise a strategy to make the most of the time you choose to invest? With the correct strategy in place, networking can help you by cutting down on time wasted looking for the right contact or information and pitching for new business. And, by building effective relationships through networking, you'll have numerous advocates for your business circulating within their own networks – surely that is worth a small investment of time?

Using the basic principles of strategic planning is an easy way to develop your networking strategy; let's look at the five components of your strategic networking plan:

Vision. Be clear on your reasons for networking and determine what your goals are, then write them down. Revisit these goals before you attend each networking event – it continues to amaze me how the law of attraction works; what you put 'out there' truly does come back to you. Don't go to events with the sole intention of making a sale or getting your business card into as many people's hands as possible. Rather, say to yourself, "I want to meet great people who will be beneficial for my soul and my career/business. I will attend each event with a smile on my face and never dismiss a person or an opportunity as unimportant or irrelevant".

Mission Statement. A mission statement is generally a short, simple statement of who you are, what product or service you provide and to whom. For the purpose of your strategic networking plan, a mission statement can help you to clarify what business you are in: for example, in Olivia's case, her mission statement might read, "In my role as sales manager I am responsible for managing my team to achieve our goals of providing cost-effective, time-saving solutions to small and medium business enterprises through the appropriate use of office machines and systems".

Critical Success Factors. Identify the tools you need to achieve success at networking events – these might include:

A clear definition of what business you are in (your'elevator statement').

Describe yourself, your business or position in a brief, concise statement – this is sometimes called an 'elevator statement' because it is short and concise enough for you to deliver between floors in an elevator. Memorise your 'elevator statement' so that when that all-important question arises, "So, what do you do?" – you are armed and ready.

Try to phrase your 'elevator statement' in terms of what benefit you deliver – rather than just what you do: for example, Olivia manages the sales department of an office machine company. Instead of simply saying, "I manage the sales department of an office machine company", she might instead say, “I am responsible for providing time-saving solutions for small and medium businesses,” or, “My team and I are responsible for saving our clients time through automation and systems” – certainly has a different ring to it, doesn’t it? A benefit-focused statement such as this also encourages further conversation and prompts the obvious next response, “Really, tell me more about that…”

A good diary system (for scheduling time to attend events).

Whether paper or electronic, use your diary effectively. Make advance diary entries for events you plan to attend, remembering to schedule the time required to travel to and from the event as well as for follow-up phone calls, coffee meetings and so on.

After each event, diarise follow up calls, reminders and advance notes about who to catch up with at the next event. There’s nothing more embarrassing or damaging to new relationships than to make a connection with a fellow guest at one event and forget their name at the next!

Systems for tracking contacts from each network and event (to keep in touch and help build relationships).

Unless you have a failsafe memory, it is beneficial to have a system for keeping track of where and when you meet people as well as a record of conversations and follow up between you. There are many database software programs available which allow you to track all relevant information and comments – try Act! or Filemaker Pro. You can track where you meet each person and use this information to look up your contacts and refresh your memory before you go to the next networking event. If you have been especially diligent about recording details in the comments field, you can make a powerful impression by picking up on conversations where you left off!

Conversation tools (to help ease the way).

Think before the event about conversation starters and icebreakers. Read the newspapers and a few business magazines to develop a bank of conversation topics, but steer clear of religion, politics and other potentially controversial subjects. You could even create an *"Oh, really?" file*, filled with interesting stories about business, science and general interest; look for stories that people will enjoy hearing or be fascinated by and want to tell others. The occasional (clean) joke never goes astray either!

Strategies and Actions.

Decide where you will network.

Evaluate the opportunities for networking. Look at industry associations, business networking groups, special interest groups and so on. The Internet is a great place to begin your search and the phone book lists industry associations.

Choose networks that fit with your interests and area of business. Create a short list of networks that you can attend regularly and that realistically fit into your monthly calendar. If your time is limited it is preferable to attend one network regularly, rather than try to spread yourself over a few networks irregularly.

Remember that networking is not only about meeting people – by attending events with guest speakers you'll get a regular motivational injection and learn something too. Networking events can also be a cost-effective and unusual way to reward your staff and thank your clients.

Maximise your involvement within each network.

Attend regularly – networking is not about meeting the greatest number of people and thrusting business cards into their hands – they will most certainly end up in the bin, it is about creating valuable and lasting business relationships.

Offer to become involved in the network through volunteering for committees, submitting articles for newsletters and websites, assisting on the registration desk or offering door prizes at events.

Arrive at events early and take the time to meet other 'early birds'. SMILE! Look approachable; no one will come near you if you have your head buried in the newspaper or look like you just swallowed the taxi driver for breakfast!

Don't be afraid to say hello, chances are the person you meet is just as nervous as you are. If you see someone standing alone looking like a nervous first-timer make the effort to draw them into your conversation and they will be thankful for the helping hand – remember Olivia and Jenny?

At sit-down events, try to sit with people you haven't met before and invite the person you met in the foyer to join you if he or she is alone. Try to get the whole table involved in a discussion; you could begin by asking everyone what brought them to the event that day. This is a great way to learn more about the motivation of each guest at your table and what they hope to achieve by attending. Take it a step further by asking what each person does – I guarantee there will be some form of synergy around the table between at least two of the guests. There really is just six degrees of separation!

Aim to make one or two great contacts at each event, anything more than that is a bonus. Look beyond their business and focus on the person. Ask for business cards if you want to stay in contact, don't wait for an offer. In my opinion it is more important that you have their business card, than that they have yours. If nothing else, it provides a great reason for you to send a follow up note with your card enclosed.

Listen to the speaker and if you have a question don't be afraid to ask it. Not only will everyone in the room see you but if you say your name and company name before you ask the question they will also know who you are. If there is no opportunity for questions, approach the speaker personally after the presentation. Speakers are just people too and they are usually very approachable and grateful for feedback.

Listen, listen and then listen some more! Treat everyone you meet with respect and integrity. Listen to the conversation and focus completely on that person. You may think that the person you are speaking with is not appropriate for your business and cannot give you anything, but who knows who that person will meet in the coming months, or who they are married to, related to, or work with? Every contact is valuable and should be treated as such. At the very least you may unearth a great person who is wonderful company!

Circulate with respect. There is nothing worse than a pushy person on a networking mission barging in on an interesting conversation and thrusting their business card into your hand – believe me, I have seen it happen many times! Be aware of body language and join the conversation politely. Wait for an appropriate moment to introduce yourself. If people are obviously engaged in a riveting conversation, don't interrupt – choose another group to speak with first.

Get to know the host. Quite often, the host of the event is a central point of contact within the network. He or she will know most of the people who attend and will have seen the name and company name of everyone in attendance through the registration process. As the host of the Businesswomen's Breakfast Series I am regularly asked if I know someone in 'X' industry or who can provide 'X' product or service.

Know when to back off with integrity. Follow your instinct – if you meet someone who doesn't 'feel right' to you, politely excuse yourself and move on. Networking is about creating valuable and meaningful associations, don't force yourself to make friends with someone you don't like or trust. There is no need to share your opinion of that person with others – just move on discretely.

Follow up and always deliver what you promise. If you promised to let a new contact know about a particular website, a good book or to send them some information, do it immediately after the event. If you didn't promise anything then a 'pleasure to meet you' note is a great idea to reinforce the connection.

If you can connect two of your contacts, then do it. Refer them freely and confidently without expectation of anything in return. Make sure that you feel comfortable recommending them to each other and that you believe each will deliver. Your colleagues and new contacts must be able to trust your judgement and value your referrals. If you have not previously worked with someone you are referring, but feel that they are trustworthy and competent, say so to the person you are referring them to and let them decide whether they choose to work together. You have simply facilitated the introduction, for which both parties will be grateful.

Bring people with you – invite new contacts from other sources as a guest to your network. If they enjoy the event they will always remember you and may even invite other colleagues who they will introduce to you. Use the event as an economical way to thank your existing clients who may in turn attend again and bring others with them.

Implementation Schedule. Decide which networks and events you will attend and plan the time in your diary well in advance. Allow time for travel to and from the venue to ensure that you arrive early and have time to continue good discussions at the end of the event.

Realise how important it is to attend each event in a positive frame of mind. If you know you will need 'wind-down' time between work and the event allow for this in your diary and de-stress with a meditation CD in the car on the way there or make time for a solo coffee beforehand.

Networking is essential for personal growth, business contacts and referrals. Treat networking as an essential part of your business strategy and not just something you do on the side, when you have time. Choose a couple of networks and for the greatest benefits, get involved as much as you can. Attend events armed with your success tools and a big smile! Don't keep score of referrals but do keep an open mind about everyone you meet. You never know who they know! Finally, follow your instincts and if someone doesn't feel right just move on without needing to discuss your reasons with anyone else.

Remember, what goes around comes around. Good luck and happy networking!

chapter three

productive networking

neen james

Networking is as much an attitude and a way of thinking as it is a skill. It is something that many people do naturally while others can find it quite daunting; but it can be learned. And when you acquire the mindset and master the skill of networking you will boost your personal productivity.

Networking requires an investment of two of your most valuable and finite resources: your time and your energy. In this chapter we will consider how you can best use these resources by choosing the most effective networking opportunities, creating systems that ensure you get the most out of every networking event and learning how to effectively engage people you meet for the first time.

Creating Connections

There are any number of different networking groups and events that you could choose to attend. To make the most effective use of your time and energy, it's worth investing effort in identifying and sampling groups that look like they might suit your personal and business needs – here's how:

Choose the network. Decide what you're looking for from a networking group and ask around. Find out what groups are available and ask for recommendations and opinions from people you respect.

Contact the network. Phone the organiser of the group or event and ask questions such as these to help you decide whether this is a good place to invest your time.

- ✦ What types of people attend this event?
- ✦ What industries are represented at this event?
- ✦ How long has this group been established?
- ✦ What three words best describe this group?
- ✦ Is there an opportunity for me to promote my business?
- ✦ Does this network have membership? If so, how does it work? What does it cost?

Visit twice before deciding to join. Allow yourself at least two opportunities to evaluate the network and to decide whether it is worth your time and energy. Sometimes your first experience may not be pleasant because you may feel nervous, so give it at least two tries.

Commit to the events. When you do find a network you enjoy, schedule the time to attend and become one of the regulars. This is a great way to establish connections with people as well as to let others get to know you.

Get involved. Volunteer to help – serving on a committee or helping with an event is a great way to get to know people: help on registration, collect business cards, offer to be the MC or help to arrange an event.

Working Networking

Getting the most out of any networking event is about more than just handing out and collecting business cards. Some people seem to think that the success of an event can be measured by the number of business cards they take away. The truth is it's better to make real connections with fewer people, rather than to pride yourself on a collection of cards that you may never use. These simple steps will help you to use your business cards effectively and to know what to do next with the cards that you collect at a networking event:

Always carry your business card. That means both in and out of business hours – even at social and sporting events; you never know when someone may need your services. Ladies, it is a good idea to keep a supply of business cards in all of your handbags while gentlemen, you may like to keep a supply in all of your coat and jacket pockets.

Never hand out cards with incorrect or crossed-out information. It is not professional. Crossed-out information may give the appearance that you are disorganised or don't pay attention to detail. Business cards are not expensive to print and you should ensure that each one you hand out is an ideal representation of you and your business.

Keep a good supply of cards. Don't allow yourself to be in a position where you can't give someone your card. Be aware of your stock and reorder before you run too low.

Ask for a business card. When you have met someone and had a conversation ask, "May I have your card?" Always ask for their card first and once you have received it then ask, "May I give you my card?" Don't assume that they will want your card; it is more polite to give it to them after they have said yes.

Ask permission. If you want to write details on someone's card (while you are still with them) always ask, "Do you mind if I make a note on the back of you card?" Some people invest substantial money in their cards and asking this question demonstrates your respect.

Write notes to yourself. When you have finished a conversation with someone, take a moment to write something about him or her on the back of his or her card. This will help jog your memory when you contact them after the event.

Schedule follow up time. Whenever I book a networking event into my diary I always schedule another 30-minute appointment with myself for the next day to follow up with the organisers and the people I meet.

When I get back to my office after an event, I gather all the cards I collected and put a rubber band around them together with note to remind me of where I met these people. I put the pile of cards on my laptop keyboard so I that I action them the next day. Some people invest in contact management systems, and many of them are good, however you can still establish an effective contact system using basic tools such as a business card holder and Microsoft Outlook or Lotus Notes.

Send handwritten cards. I handwrite thank you cards to those people I made a real connection with. I thank them for the time we spent, for the information they gave me or acknowledge some other connection that we made. Receiving a handwritten card in the mail is so unusual and personal that it delivers with it a powerful impression, far stronger than a quick email might.

Book a 20-minute coffee. If you have connected with someone at an event and you want to know more about him or her and their business, make an appointment with them for a 20-minute coffee. Twenty minutes is an easy appointment for most people to fit into their schedules. It indicates that while you are interested in finding out more about them, you also value their time. When you contact them you might say,

"I'd like to invite you for a 20-minute coffee to find out more about what you do, what day is most suitable for you?" Make sure you honour the 20 minutes. At the 20-minute mark I always stop the meeting and say, "I promised it would only take 20 minutes, so thank you for your time". At this point the person you are with is able to choose whether they want to end the meeting or continue.

Send a thank you to the event organiser. Take the time to thank the organisers of the event, let them know why you found it valuable and include your business card in the envelope. A great deal of time and energy goes into organising events and people appreciate you taking the time to acknowledge that.

Creating Impactful Business Cards

One of the most important tools for any networking event is your business card. A good business card is crucial; it creates the first impression when you hand it to someone and is a lasting reminder of you and your business every time they look at it. What does your business card say about you?

Your business card is not only your calling card but also your 'pocket billboard'; invest in creating an impactful card that helps people to connect with who you are and what your business is. You might do this by:

- ✦ including a photo of yourself or your business
- ✦ creating a tear-apart card so that a person can keep one half and pass the other on to a friend
- ✦ choosing an interesting paper stock or using striking colours that reflect your logo or image
- ✦ creating a folded card with a photo and story about your business on the inside.

When I first began in the speaking business I created a foldout card using an unusual sparkly paper stock. The colours I used were pink and purple, my corporate colours. Everyone who takes my card comments on its design, colour or feel. I consider the initial expense of design and production as an investment in creating a memorable representation of my business.

However creative you choose to make your business card, ensure that it adheres to some basics of good design and good manners:

- Make sure your name and telephone number stand out. Consider using a larger or bolder typeface for these key details. It helps people to locate your contact information quickly and also helps those who wear glasses, as they won't need to reach for them just to read your card.
- Don't forget about the back of your card – it's a wasted opportunity to communicate if left blank. Use the space to promote your business or to provide useful tips for your customers.

- ✦ It is wise to work to a standard business card size so that people can file your card and access your details easily.

Look at other people's business cards for ideas and inspiration and speak with your designer about creating something memorable for you. Ask for feedback on your concepts and designs from a variety of people to get a feel for how different people react to your card before you settle on a design.

Meeting and Greeting

When you have decided to attend an event or join a network, another important skill is knowing how to engage people when you first meet them. Meeting new people and making conversation can be daunting, but with a few simple techniques such as those listed below and some insights into how to create a great first impression from Robyn Henderson (see box) you'll become more and more comfortable with each new event.

Appear confident. There's an element of 'fake it until you make it' here. Smile when you first meet someone and look him or her in the eye. Even if you don't feel it, your smile and eye contact will show the other person that you are friendly and confident.

Be aware of your body language. Be aware of good posture; stand straight with your shoulders back. Don't fidget with pens or your clothing – keep your hands by your side if you are someone who constantly fidgets. A smile, combined with good posture will boost your confidence.

Introduce yourself first. Rather than stand alone, be brave. Walk up to an individual, or a group, extend your hand and say, "Hi, my name is Neen James, nice to meet you". Everyone will respond positively to your confidence and appreciate you making the first move. It will be a trigger for others to do the same.

Shake hands. This is an important skill; if you don't know how to shake hands properly, learn. Some women, particularly those who haven't been required to do it in business, can lack confidence with their handshake. It's important. Cultivate a firm handshake – not too hard, but just right. Look the person in the eye when you shake their hand and say their name, "Hi Robyn, it's nice to meet you". If you are unsure about whether or not to shake hands with someone, extend your hand first. It is rude to not shake the hand of someone who offers his or hers to you.

Learn how to pronounce their name. When you encounter someone with a difficult to pronounce name, ask him or her to repeat it, spell it and say it again – and allow him or her to correct your pronunciation so you get it right. People will appreciate you taking the time to learn how to say their name properly.

Use a person's name several times when you first meet. This will help you to remember their name, it is a very personal way to communicate – and, people love the sound of their own name!

Learn conversational skills. The ability to make conversation is what scares so many people about new social interactions, here a few questions you can ask anyone you meet for the first time:

- What do you do?
- Where do you work?
- Where do you live? Does it take you long to get from home to the office?
- What inspires you?
- What do you like to read?
- What has been your most valuable business lesson?

Ask people what they like to do in their spare time. This is a great question and most people become energised when you ask them about their life outside of work. Watch their eyes sparkle as they tell you about the activities they most enjoy. Take the time to discover that people are far more interesting than their work.

If you meet someone with an accent, ask where he or she is from. Find out something interesting about their country by asking:

- ✦ Where are you from?
- ✦ How often do you go to visit?
- ✦ What do you miss most about that place?
- ✦ Who is someone famous from there?
- ✦ What food is that country famous for?

If you are at an industry or charity event, ask how they heard about the event. It's a great icebreaker and allows you both to share stories about how you came to be at the event and what you hope to achieve by attending.

Listen intently. Give the person you are speaking with your full attention. Use active listening techniques such as nodding, smiling and leaning towards them while they speak. Ask questions about the topics you are discussing. People will appreciate your attention. It is very rude to look beyond the person you are speaking with or to look around the room for someone more interesting.

Effective networking can help you to maximise your productivity. You can master networking by choosing how you invest your time and energy. Choose your networks wisely, be prepared with business cards, follow up after every event, be engaging when you meet people…and have fun!

chapter four

how to win friends and interest people:

tips for making a great impression

robyn henderson

To interest people, ... you have to be interesting

What are the characteristics of interesting or charismatic people? Is there any advantage in working on becoming more interesting? From a networker's perspective, the answer is a most resounding 'yes'. People do business with people they know, like and trust; interesting people attract others easily and need to expend far less energy selling their product or services or fast-tracking their careers. So how can you become more interesting?

Become a storyteller. Interesting people are often good at telling stories. They shorten their yarns into anecdotes brought alive with enthusiasm and have a way of turning a negative into a positive, even if it is just to remind us how lucky we are in that moment. People recall stories that trigger emotions – whether happy or sad.

Be sincere. People can sense a fraud a mile away. We all know those people who are just being nice to us because they want something.

Research your interests. The Internet has opened up the information world and search engines make it incredibly easy to access information about almost anything. Visit Ask Jeeves, www.aj.com, Jeeves can answer just about any question you can create, no matter how obscure.

Get focused. Write a list of 20 things you would be interested in doing if you had a month off and an unlimited budget – let your imagination take hold. Your list might include some old hobbies, new interests and maybe even more of what you are currently doing.

Move out of your comfort zone. Too many people sit back and wait for life to happen – and they end up waiting for a long time. Proactive people are the ones who make life happen; try new things, even if they scare you a little.

Attend a special course. So many people think that networking has to be work related. In fact, some of the best contacts you will make will be in social or special-interest settings. If you can't commit to long-term studies, try one of the many short courses offered by local community colleges – what a great way to network.

Get great at introducing yourself

Becoming a more interesting person is just the beginning – you not only need to be more interesting, but to sound more interesting – you need to be able to engage and inspire people about who you are and show them that you are someone worth knowing. If you're already attending business networks, handing out your business cards, doing the follow up and getting no results, it could be that you are sabotaging yourself through the language that you use.

Research shows that we have less than 30 seconds to really make an impression when we first meet someone. You might look good, buy flattering clothes and make all the right moves, but if your language is letting you down, if your voice quavers every time you introduce yourself to someone, your credibility will be lost and you'll have to network far harder than someone who communicates their value instantly.

Let's take a look at some of the introductions that I have heard in recent months from people who at first appear to be well-dressed professionals, and who I might have considered doing business with, or at least introducing to someone in my network who might have done business with them. My thought responses to their introductions are shown in brackets. Then I've proposed how they might have more interestingly and confidently introduced themselves, and how I might have responded instead.

Did say:

"I'm just a junior partner..."

(Well, sounds like I had better wait until I meet the senior partner before I give my business to your firm.)

Could have said:

"I'm a junior partner with 'X' – we are true innovators in the areas of 'abc' and 'xyz'. You may have seen our firm written up in last Thursday's Financial Review?"

(This person really sounds like he knows what he's doing – I wonder if he has room for another client?)

Did say:

"I've just started my small business. I'm, um, a designer, a graphic designer, but I am finding it really tough to get things happening..."

(Sounds a bit too vague to me, not quite sure what he does, can't be any good or he would be busy – I think I will steer clear for now and let someone else find out if he's any good or not.)

Could have said:

"I'm a graphic designer, I specialise in corporate logos, advertisements, websites – anything that corporates need to make them look good and be memorable. I work for myself now, after 15 years in the industry, and find that I can now give my clients the one-on-one service that is missing in the marketplace today."

(One-on-one – that's what I need, someone who understands me, quick get his card!)

Did say:

"I'm just a graduate with 'X', they don't let me near any clients yet, just put me in the back room to do all the support stuff. I'm really good at what I do though. I topped my class at uni."

(If you were that good they would let you out in the marketplace, I don't think so…I won't follow up with this one – not experienced enough yet.)

Could have said:

"I work with 'X', they headhunted me as I topped my class at uni. They realise that even though I am only 25, I have a lot to offer the organisation and the client base. We specialise in creating…"

(Wow, what a bright young person, she will really go far – good on her, it's great to see a 25- year-old with that much confidence. I must connect her with a few of the movers and shakers here tonight.)

If you are guilty of self-sabotaging through your own negative introductions start practising a new script today – even if you have to write out your introduction and repeat it again and again until it rolls off your tongue. Leave out negative words such as: but, no worries, can't, won't, might, try.

The bottom line is if you don't value yourself, how can you expect anyone else to value you?

You will be surprised how easily and well people will respond to you when you start to value your own worth.

Write your introduction here:

chapter five

the habits of good networking

sue henry

As a small business coach and owner, I've learnt that networking can provide outstanding results in your life, career and business. But it's not an ad-hoc activity; effective networking is something that you have to continually work at. Using networking to leverage business requires good habits and a simple, practical system. I use a system that supports my natural style, which makes creating lasting networking habits easy. It includes a combination of habit tracking and checking, together with a well-managed database which enables me to keep in touch regularly through face-to-face visits, phone calls, emails, invitations, newsletters and letters. This simple system can also help you to create and maintain networking habits that suit your personality and business.

The basics of establishing good networking habits

Know what you want to achieve and what might stand in your way.

I have clients who express real fears when it comes to networking – they perceive themselves to be poor networkers or not good at functions and small talk. The fact is, networking is not about small talk at all – it is a life skill that will help you to make connections with people to whom you can be of service and who may in turn be of service to you.

Take some time to think about what networking means to you. Draw a line down the centre of a clean page; on the left note all the fears and anxieties that networking brings up for you. Now think about the people you know who are good networkers, and for each fear write down how those people would handle the situation. Identify the networking habits you would like to develop and make a note of these.

Start with something simple and practice it daily.

For the first three weeks, start creating the networking habit of calling two people every day. This one activity will bring many unexpected results and it will only take a few minutes. Once you've mastered this networking habit, introduce another.

Track and monitor your progress.

At the end of each day take a few minutes to think about your networking and record your thoughts, learnings and wins. Ask yourself, what worked, what didn't and how you can improve? Using a networking habit tracker can help you to see your progress while acting as a daily reminder of what you need to do. Download a daily networking tracker from www.smallbusinessaccelerator.com/tracker.pdf.

Now let's look at the system tools and techniques in more detail

The database

The database is the key to this system. A good database, kept up to date, and used to build and maintain relationships can be an invaluable source of new opportunities, repeat business and resources.

Maintaining your database is imperative. I keep a special box in my office into which I put people's business cards as soon as I return from an event or meeting, and I have a rule that within 24 hours of meeting someone new, I enter their details into the database together with a note about where I met them and what is unique about them. I then use a contact cycle to make sure that I connect with people on a regular basis. Over time, I record details about all of our interactions and what I learn about their needs and what is important to them.

People often ask me what type of database they should keep. The simple answer is – it depends on your needs. I have one client who keeps his records on a manual card system, others keep a simple spreadsheet, and some have advanced software. I use a software solution that interacts with my handheld electronic diary so that I can immediately access phone numbers and email addresses and make notes.

Face-to-face visits

I love face-to-face visits, especially when we usually rely so heavily on email to communicate with our customers these days.

In the early days of my business I was left without Internet access for almost a full week; I felt like I had been cut off from the business world. At first I was annoyed at the inconvenience, but decided that if I was going to be stuck with so much down time I would make the most of it; I decided to embark on a relationship-building and fact-finding mission – using old-fashioned face-to-face visits. I called several customers and organised meetings, lunches, coffees and even a round of golf. I was mindful that these people were giving up their valuable time to meet with me so before each meeting I gave thought to how I could provide value to them so that their time would be well invested. During that week I spent invaluable time with my customers and had the opportunity to ask questions and develop a unique understanding of their businesses, their challenges and their needs. And in more cases than not, I benefited from unexpected information or new business.

Taking time to visit with my customers, associates and other contacts is now an integral part of my business. I make a point of scheduling time in my diary and meeting with at least one person every day. This one habit has led to many business opportunities.

Maintaining phone contact

I make it a rule to contact two people by phone every day (no exceptions!). These can be customers, business associates, suppliers, contacts or potential customers. This simple habit has helped me to maintain my contacts and increased the amount of referral business that I receive.

I first started using the 'two-call' system when I was learning how to sell; I found that by scheduling just two calls per day I didn't feel overwhelmed at the thought of having to make lots of sales calls and, I reasoned, at worst it was only going to take five minutes!

I plan my calls at the start of the day and usually call between 11am and 3pm – this respects the fact that most people are busy when they first arrive at work and are thinking about what has to be done after hours or trying to get away towards end of the day.

I open the conversation by identifying myself and reminding the person of where we met, then I ask *"if now is a good time to talk?"*, and state the reason for my call:

"I'm following up on a conversation we had at 'X' function..."

"I thought we could organise to get together and discuss business opportunities..."

"I'm interested in finding out more about what you do..."

"I would love to meet up so that I can get to know more about you..."

"I'm organising a lunch with like-minded people and I thought you might like to come along..."

If I'm not sure about what to say, I use something along the lines of,

"I'm working on developing my networking skills and have met some really interesting people – when I met you I thought you would be a great person to meet up with for coffee so I thought I'd contact you..."

Email contact

I once read that you cannot service too much and this has been a guide to the way I use email in my business. Before I send each email I ask, 'Will this information be of service to 'X'?' The email may be a newsletter, an interesting piece of information, a quote, an article of interest, an idea, survey or even just a quick hello.

I don't know the magic formula for how much is too much with email communication – what I do know is what my customers like, and I only know this by asking them and getting to know them better.

There are a few simple rules that I follow when sending emails:

- I never include an attachment unless the recipient is expecting it – I've found that attachments can be mistaken for viruses or be too large for the recipient's inbox.
- I keep emails short and to the point.
- I clearly describe my message in the subject line (for example, Touching base, Let's meet for coffee, Information you might find interesting, Following up).
- If I want a reply, I request it in the content of the message.
- I always include my contact details when signing off the email.

Invitations

I have often taken clients and networking contacts to functions and events and have found that this gives me the opportunity to get to know them a lot better, share a common interest and discuss opportunities. I always make a point of sending invitations with as much notice as possible so that the person receiving it has sufficient time to respond and to schedule the event in their diary.

Newsletters

Newsletters are an excellent way to maintain regular contact with your networks – I include friends and family on my mailing list, which has been a great way for me to reach a much wider audience as they often send the newsletter on to their contacts. Newsletters can also be a great conversation piece when you meet someone new: "I have a newsletter that goes out monthly reporting on 'X', would you like me to send you the last one so you can see if you'd like to join the mailing list?"

Letters with interesting pieces of information

I often scan newspapers and magazines for articles, stories and case studies that I can send to my contacts; it shows that you have taken the time to think about their business and what might be of interest to them. I send the article, together with a handwritten note, and have found that this is a great way to build rapport, develop relationships as well as to remind people of who I am and what my business is about.

Words of Networking Advice

I follow five guiding networking principles and I believe that these are the major contributors to my networking success and they can be yours too:

1. ***Budget time and money.*** I allocate a budget for networking, including phone calls, emails, postage, events, conferences, lunches and coffee meetings. The networking budget is included in my overall sales and marketing budget. Monitoring how I spend my networking budget helps me to determine what to invest when planning each year's networking activities.

2. ***Curiosity killed the cat, not the successful networker.*** Always be curious, the more you learn about others the better positioned you will be to have access to all that you desire! I've learnt that silence is golden; by asking good questions, maintaining eye contact and remaining present in the conversation, I can control the conversation, learn more about the person I am speaking with and be alert for any opportunities that might arise.

3. ***Loose lips sink ships.*** Always maintain your integrity and sincerity. Take a genuine interest in people and be clear about your intentions when networking. Give compliments freely and sincerely – but never when you don't mean them. If you are given information in confidence, keep it that way. The quickest way to ruin your reputation and your business is to betray a confidence.

4. ***Turn your mobile phone off.*** Turning off your mobile phone allows you to be present in the moment and shows respect for the organisers and other attendees

5. ***Enjoy what you do and keep it fun.*** I believe this is one of the most critical factors. Do what you love and love what you do! Sales and marketing, training, workshops and interacting with people every day are what I love, which makes it easy for me to network with my customers, associates and potential customers.

chapter six

networking: the skill of friendship

lee-anne carson

Everything I need to know I learnt in the sandbox.

I watched one day as my 12-month-old son, Richard, made strangers into friends in the sandbox. Today, seven years later, one of the boys Richard met that day is still one of his best friends. How? Had my son, at the age of just one, mastered the skill of networking?

At just 12 months of age Richard had:

- looked around the yard for what he wanted to do
- decided that it was the sandbox and looked for a spot where he might fit in
- made eye contact and said "hello" to those near him
- joined in with what the others were doing

- took turns with the toys
- included those around him when he wanted to play a new game
- put the toys back where he had found them, ready for the next day.

Richard had learnt:

- to share everything
- to include everyone (you wouldn't want to be left out)
- that everyone is your friend (so play fair)
- to say you're sorry if you do hurt someone
- not to take what is not yours
- to leave on good terms (so they'll want to play with you tomorrow).

Not an exhaustive list, but a pretty good foundation for networking; it seems simple enough, so why do I make it so hard for myself every day? The process of networking follows the same 'sandbox' format: the decision, the introduction, playing together and having something to look forward to.

The decision

You have to decide you want to play in the sandbox; that you want to network, make friends and be 'out there'. The first step is your decision.

Make a list of all the business and community organisations you're interested in joining:

- Why do they attract you?
- What sets them apart and why do individuals attend?
- How are they structured: breakfast, lunch, evening?
- What do you hope to get out of attending or belonging?
- Are there Internet networking groups that you can join which bring the same benefits?
- Are there any competitive businesses in the group and does this make any difference to whether or not you join?

Take the time to investigate and attend a few meetings until you decide on the one or two groups that you want to invest your time and effort in. Then, like Richard in the sandbox, jump in with enthusiasm!

The introduction

A friendly smile and "hello" is a good beginning... but it does need to be backed up by a few sentences.

If you know who you are going to met, do some research on their work, expertise and interests. Focus the first three minutes of your conversation on topics that they would enjoy discussing. If you don't know who you might meet, read up on current issues and recent events that are relevant to the location you are going to, or to the group function you are attending. Begin with a conversation-starting comment and then ask a question. Develop a few quality questions that require responses of more than a just a few words. Think of it like a game of volleyball – you set up the serve and pass the ball to them.

Body gestures are powerful communicators and maintaining eye contact with the person you are speaking with is critical. Focus on them as though they are the only person in the room. There is nothing worse than speaking with someone who is pretending to listen to you while their eyes are searching the room for their next 'victim' or for someone more important than you. Each person you speak with is important, valuable and extraordinary; find the diamond in everyone. You'll never know the treasure of who they are, who they know or how they might help you unless you are sincerely interested in them as a unique person.

Be aware of other body gestures such as having an engaging smile, an upbeat tone of voice and keeping your arms relaxed by your sides or animated when speaking to demonstrate you are open and receptive. Remember to smile. It costs nothing, enriches those you are speaking with and although it happens in a flash, it is remembered forever.

Repeat the other person's name in your conversation, and they will remember yours. Be a good listener; encourage them to talk about themselves and remember what they have said (you might need to write it down afterwards to make sure you do remember).

Ask a few people who you trust to give you feedback on how you come across.

Playing together

Drop an email or send a handwritten note within 24 hours of meeting someone new. Mention something special that you spoke about and create a reason to get together again. An ideal reason is to introduce a few of your new contacts to others whom they may wish to meet over lunch; build a reputation for being someone who helps to connect people.

Be genuinely interested in the other person – be sincere in making them feel they are important and they will return the favour.

Theme your networking based on a paraphrased version of John F Kennedy's famous speech: "Ask not what they can do for you, ask what you can do for them".

Something to look forward to

Frequent and meaningful contact is the best way to deepen a relationship. Just as any relationship is two-way, give the other person time to respond and reciprocate. New friendships made through networking are built over time and through mutual respect; act needy and you will be treated with disdain and avoided. Ensure your communication leaves the other person feeling liked, not nagged.

Create a 'brightness of the future' reason for getting in touch again. 'Brightness of the future' translates into the Four Cs of Networking:

1. **Commonality** – find a common connection
2. **Compelling** – be bold, confident and have a love for life
3. **Communication** – keep in touch consistently and creatively
4. **Caring** – be sincerely interested in the other person and their interests

Ten Secrets to the 'Inner Circle'

When I was ten years old, my father told me: "To have friends, you need to be a friend". I was struggling at the time in a three-way best-friend relationship: whoever was on the 'out' at the time struggled to prove they were better than either of the two who were 'in' and to re-win best-friend status with one of them – thereby forcing someone else into the 'out'. The trouble was we were each focussed on ourselves. The moment I stopped struggling to be 'better', and focussed instead on what each of the other two girls wanted, I become both of their best friends!

After that I focussed on others rather than myself. I helped others to reach their goals and thereby built a support network that helped me to reach mine. The old adage proved to be true: 'It's not what you know, it's who you know' – it continues to be true today, and has made all the difference.

These are my ten secrets to the acquisition and cultivation of influential connections, or what I call the 'inner circle'.

Secret 1: Know what you want

What are your aspirations? Do you want to be CEO of a Top 100 company? Prime Minister? Known for your philanthropy? The most respected person in your field? Whatever it is, you won't get there by chance. You need to know who it is you need to know, and for what reason.

Who in history has done what you want to do? Read their biographies and understand what they did to get there. Who is currently in the same or a similar role to that which you want to be in? Who are the most important players? Map out what their path was. What clubs and organisations did they belong to? What additional skills did they have that you might need to acquire?

Research, research and more research. Know what you want. Know what you need to do.

Secret 2: Build it and they will come

I collect lists of the people I want to meet. I write their names down in a book, together with their picture so that I will recognise them at an event or chance meeting. My lists are made up from the 'Top 50 Under 40', the '100 Most Influential People in Business', the 'Top 10 CEOs' – the 'movers and shakers' who have been recognised as being at the top of their field or as an up-and-comer to keep an eye on. These are the people I want to surround myself with. These are the people I want to learn from and emulate.

It is amazing how the universe will support you once you put your desire down on paper: at a conference I was impressed by an influential speaker who had expressed the same concerns that I wanted to write about in a book. After she spoke I went up to her and said, "You just wrote my book" – I asked her if I could call to discuss her speech further. She agreed and we met for coffee a few days later. We discussed how my writing might be best suited to a series of articles for a specific magazine. I agreed, but at the time I had no idea how that would happen – so I put the editors of the magazine down on my list of those people I wanted to meet. The next day I received an email inviting me to a breakfast where those editors happened to be speaking and I would have the opportunity to be introduced to them!

Write down the names of the people you want to meet and it is amazing what happens.

When you meet someone on your list celebrate in the book with stars and write special comments about them such as their children's names, husband's or wife's name, special interests and most importantly – the common thread that will allow you to keep in touch.

While I was creating a list of people I wanted to know, I figured that other people were probably doing the same; I got myself into the 'Who's Who' and 'The Celebrity Book' so people could find me too.

Secret 3: Build it before you need it

Eighty percent of networking is about keeping in touch. Make a habit of thoughtfully calling or emailing 25 people per day. The call or email must be meaningful to the other person. Relationships take time. Build your relationships with others one call at a time, one coffee at a time, one chance meeting at a time. It takes seven meaningful contacts per year to be remembered. If you are not remembered others cannot refer you or recommend you.

Stephen Covey introduced the concept of an 'emotional bank account' in relationships. I agree entirely with this concept. Like bank accounts, over time you make small deposits into relationships until one day you need to make a withdrawal. I make sure, in all my relationships, that I deposit far more time, effort, listening and support than I ever withdraw or ask for. I never know when the time might come that I need to make a big withdrawal or ask for a favour. I don't want to be caught with 'no money in the account' – for the person to feel that I am asking too much from the relationship or 'using them'.

Secret 4: Don't keep score

Give; give freely and keep giving. As you reach out, giving to others and depositing in that 'emotional bank account', the relationship will grow and the network will grow. Their network will become your network. As your network grows, your net worth will grow.

Networking is not all about getting what you want; it's about ensuring that everyone you care about gets what they want too. The best networking is when you can connect two people who don't know each other but should. It is not about keeping score of how much you have done for someone and how much time, effort or value you gave. Think of it like 'career karma' – what you give out will come back to you tenfold. Networking is a personal connection that both parties feel good about and want to reciprocate in the future. The strength of your network derives as much from the diversity of the people you know as well as the quality and quantity.

Secret 5: Everyone is important

You never know who that quiet person in the corner is or who the receptionist in the company you are calling on is married to. I've learnt this over and over in my life.

Once while waiting for a meeting, I was asked by a smartly dressed woman if I would like tea or coffee. Fortunately I looked her in the eye, smiled, and engaged in polite and friendly conversation. To my surprise, when I entered the boardroom, I learnt that she was the CEO. On another occasion, I was at a large gathering wanting to meet a certain executive but not knowing what he looked like. I saw a group of very distinguished individuals all swarming around a very important looking person who I assumed was the executive. My eye caught an unassuming individual off to the side of the throng. I smiled and we struck up a friendly conversation laughing at the growing swarm of people in front of us. The unassuming individual asked me, "Did you wish to meet him?" of course I said yes and he said, "Fine, I am his personal secretary, you can have a private meeting with him in 20 minutes in his suite." With that, both the executive and his secretary left the room and the throng behind – and I had my private audience.

Once when I asked why I had won a particular piece of business, the senior contact said, "We always ask our receptionist how she is treated and how the companies behave in the foyer. We believe your behaviour when we are not looking is how we can expect to be treated as a company in the long term".

Secret 6: Be known, but be known for something

Being know and respected for a talent, expertise or uniqueness is much better than just being known. It is the depth of your talent or expertise that is important. It's like thinking of yourself as a 'brand' – when people say your name, what are the five words they would use to describe you. Is there consistency in what different people think of you? Is it what you want to be said about you and what you want to be known for? Perception drives reality. Create the perception you want others to have of you through your actions. Be interesting for others to be interested in you. Do the little things that make a big impression – a magnetic smile, a firm handshake, a listening ear and a personality that says, 'I'm excited about life!'

Secret 7: There is no harm in asking

Fear is the belief in something not true. Every person you want to meet has been in the same situation as you. Everyone has had to ask for something they want. If you get a 'no', it only means you are closer to a 'yes'. Keep going.

Secret 8: Nurture levels

We all have our peer groups – we gather, lunch and do social activities together. Find someone in your group who has a friend 'two levels higher' than your peer group, and invite that person to join a luncheon or social activity with your peer group. The 'two levels higher' person becomes a 'stepping stone' into a new peer group. Nurture this new person and create fabulous social engagements that they want to invite their friends to. It sounds crass to talk about the process in this way but if you are mixing good fun, lively conversation, interesting connections and beneficial encounters then they are usually happy to attend. The next step is to mentor someone and become a 'stepping stone' for them.

Secret 9: Be seen

Getting out there is half the battle. Frequent interactions and those small moments of recognition will keep you at the top of their minds and on the tips of their tongues when an opportunity arises. Invisibility is worse than failure. 'Be seen to be known' is an old saying that continues to hold true even in this age of electronic interactions. We trust those people who we know and many of us need to know people by meeting them in the flesh.

Think about wearing something that creates an instant recognition, such as always wearing a bow tie if you are a man or always something in the colour pink if you are a woman.

Plan to use 25 per cent of your time developing contacts in a social environment, at conferences or events. Never have breakfast or lunch alone. You have to eat – and what better way to keep your contacts current than to plan a 'frequency of contact' program that includes breakfasts, lunches, afternoon coffee or drinks.

Secret 10: Where to go to be seen

Scour your three main communities – where you live, the industry you work in and your current circle of friends. What groups do you want to belong to that will get you to where you want to go? Choose one group or organisation from each of the three communities you participate in.

Do more than join a networking group or an organisation. Getting involved in volunteer committees, holding office, giving of your time and contributing are excellent ways to raise your profile.

Offer to speak at every conference you can. Develop your expertise in various subjects and in public speaking. When you are at the front of the room, you are meeting everyone in the room – make an offer that they can come and speak to you about for further information.

Sit on the board of a not-for-profit organisation. If you are serious about advancing in life, choose a charity that touches your heart and give of your time and effort.

Attend political fundraisers – this is where money and passion meet.

Sit in first class in airplanes. The people you want to know sit there. The most receptive time to start a conversation is when you are both eating – food is always a good conversation starter.

Make a difference. Consciously construct what you want in your life. Explore, listen, learn, listen, connect, listen, give, give and give some more. Have a relentless focus on what you want in your life. Networking works because everyone knows they will need something or someone at some time. The people you want to know have done exactly the same thing before you.

chapter seven

turning perfect strangers into advocates

robyn henderson

Many of us are familiar with the steps on the customer 'ladder of loyalty' and the process of turning suspects into advocates. A similar process can be applied to networking – turning strangers into advocates.

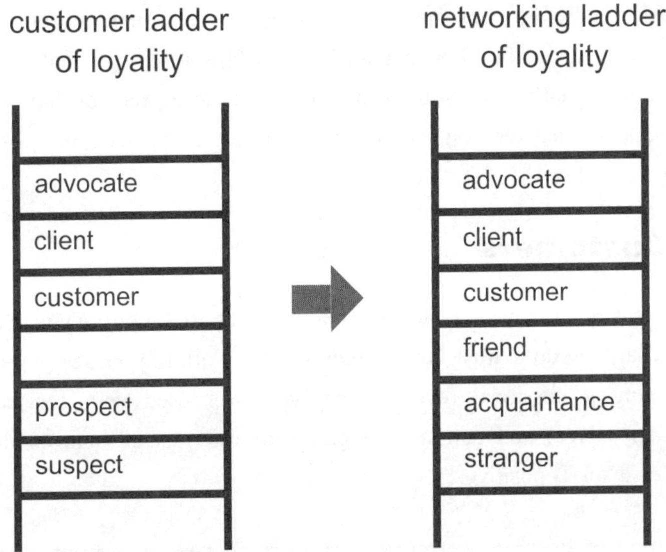

Strangers

In the networking world, strangers are friends-in-waiting – we just haven't met them yet.

Acquaintances

We make someone's acquaintance when we make contact or are introduced; this can happen face-to-face, electronically over the phone or by fax.

Friends

Friends are the big difference between the customer ladder of loyalty and the networking ladder of loyalty. Networkers become friends before they become customers. We're not necessarily talking about building personal friendships (although that does happen) but about forming the basis of a caring relationship and realising that everyone you meet is an interesting person, not just a potential order.

Customers

A customer may never actually place an order or buy from you. But what they do is trust you enough to refer work to you, see you as being professional (even if they've never used your services themselves) and continue to give you referrals as long as the feedback is positive.

Clients

A client is anyone who buys twice…and continues to buy from you either personally or through continued referrals.

Advocates

Advocates love you and are your most loyal supporters; they love the fact that you remember the names of their partner and children, and their birthdays. And they are more than impressed that you remembered they were having their wisdom tooth out last month and cared enough to ask about it. They love the little newspaper clippings you send them from time to time about their obscure passion. You amaze them with your memory and recall of past conversations – sometimes they think you must write all their stuff down; how else could you remember it all? They put the postcard you sent them while you were on holidays on their notice board and constantly ask you for more business cards as they refer more and more business to you. They are your advocate because they believe you truly care about them and you make them feel special.

chapter eight

how to generate endless referrals

robyn henderson

Effective networking is about more than just showing up – the point is to be remembered positively and to know how to turn business cards into business and a regular stream of referrals.

Why is it that if two people regularly attend the same networking function, one might quickly get known while the other is barely acknowledged by a handful of people? What is the missing ingredient? In the networking environment the people who are remembered are the ones who:

- follow up when they say they will
- refer business to others regularly
- promise good and deliver great – constantly exceeding people's expectations

- connect people they meet with people they can do business with
- generously share information
- believe in the networking concept that there is plenty for everyone: plenty of business, plenty of money, plenty of opportunities and plenty of ideas.

People who meet all of these criteria become spheres of influence. Spheres of influence are people who know a little bit about a lot of things, and a lot about one or two things. They are very generous in sharing information, very good at remembering what is important to you and very good at keeping in touch. They have generally earned the respect of their peers and networks and are trusted by many. Spheres of influence are the people many companies try to attract to endorse their products. They always work with integrity and are rarely seen endorsing something or someone they do not believe in. What would it take to make you a sphere of influence and build a positive profile in your company or community?

Let's start with a list of networking habits that will systematically and affordably help you to build your profile.

Profile-Building Strategies

- Some businesses make the mistake of only networking when they have no orders in the in-tray; this is too late. You might receive some business straight away, but most business will take time to develop, if you are continually networking, you will never run out of work. Make a commitment to spending 15 minutes per day involved in some networking activity and to attend one networking function each week – within six to eight weeks, you will start to see substantial results.

- Exchange a minimum of twenty-five business cards every week.

- Send a thank you card to someone every day including some to non-work related people who may have helped you in some way.

- Attend at least one networking function every week; be prepared to try new or different networks, preferably ones where there are a lot of new faces.

- Consider becoming involved in a committee that you are genuinely interested in; it may be sport, the arts, the environment, politics, wherever your interests lie. In the short term you might offer to help out on the registration desk, or with 'meeting and greeting'. Wear a nametag, introduce yourself to others, and find out how you can help people. You don't have to do it for the rest of your life, and who knows, you may even enjoy it. More importantly you'll be networking with decision makers and people who are making things happen.

- ✦ Develop a win/win relationship with your printer. It is important that all of your business stationery and promotional materials reflect the image you want to create. If you are starting out in business with a limited budget find a reliable printer who can discuss all of your requirements with you and help you to introduce new items as your business grows. Many people make the mistake of outlaying a lot of money on fantastic promotional materials that they don't use wisely, leaving them instead on the shelf because of courier or postage costs or saving them only for definite customers. Distribute your materials widely to targeted audiences to increase your profile.

- ✦ Find a good webmaster who understands your business, your budget and the message you want to deliver, with whom you can develop a lasting relationship. Technology enables us to reach many people quickly and affordably. It is important that your website reflects your message and your image. Ask trusted friends (and a stranger or two) to give you honest feedback on the message that your promotional material conveys. Is it congruent with the message you want to send? Are you fun loving and carefree yet working with a very conservative website? Are you sending mixed messages?

✦ Remember people's birthdays. Birthdays are generally fun days and are everyone's one special day in the year. Remembering clients' birthdays is a thoughtful, low cost reason to keep in touch. How do you find out someone's birthday? Ask them. Many businesses ask people to fill in application forms that include their date of birth, so you might already have access to this information. Note that you are asking for the person's birthday, not date of birth. Some people are very guarded about their age but will happily reveal their birthday. Again technology comes to the rescue with birthday reminders. All you have to do is ask the question, when is your birthday?

- Running a Melbourne Cup sweep for your clients is a great way of being remembered positively. The week before the race prepare a budget for the prizes and a list of clients who will receive a runner in the race. Prizes might include a dinner for two, movie tickets, wine, flowers – whatever suits your budget. On the day before the race, prepare the sweep; make a call to each client advising them which horse they have drawn and what the prizes are. Follow up the next day with congratulations to the winners. Be warned, this is usually so well received that it may become an annual event for you!

- Retailers are always looking for something new to draw customers into their outlets. At Easter you might give a small Easter egg to everyone who comes into your store. Be prepared, ideas like this are well received and usually get talked about in the community. It is sometimes best to restrict these promotions to 'while stocks last' in case you generate a rush. One newsagent I know has red frog day every Monday. Anyone who makes a purchase over $3 on a Monday receives a red frog (a little sugary sweet). He is located in a central business area and it is not surprising that Monday is one of his best days. A boutique I know does not discount clothing, however, they have a policy whereby anyone who purchases garments over $250 receives a complimentary pair of earrings and anyone who purchases over $500 receives a scarf or belt. A restaurant within a large club gives a free lunch to anyone having a birthday – do you think many people celebrate their birthday alone? Not usually, their record is a booking for 25 people – all as a result of one complimentary meal. Don't be afraid to try things that haven't been done in your industry before – just because they haven't been done doesn't mean they won't work.

- Some people use postcards for all of their networking correspondence. Postcards can be particularly effective because they immediately stand out from the rest of the daily mail and provide enough space for just a short message (you also save on the costs of envelopes). The front of the card might be a photo, cartoon, drawing or something related to your business. Since relocating my business to the far north coast of New South Wales I have started a hobby of taking photos of sunrises and have hundreds of beautiful sunrise photos that I have made into postcards. I had a sticker made to attach to the back of each photo advising of my change of address details, mentioning my new hobby and providing enough space for me to write a small handwritten note. The feedback from these postcards has been very positive. Sunrises are not something that everyone makes the effort to see and I love sharing them. If you would like to receive a sunrise postcard, email me at **robyn@networkingtowin.com.au** and include your postal address.

✦ My inbox bulges with over 200 emails every day, and I forward lots of emails on to people who might be interested in them. Yet for me, nothing beats the personal touch and the fact that someone has taken the time to send something that they believe might be relevant, useful or helpful to me. At least once a week I buy international newspapers to keep me up to date with global trends (international and interstate newspapers are often available at newsagents, capital city airports and many five star hotels, plus you can subscribe electronically to daily news summaries to keep in touch with what's happening around the globe). I read the papers cover to cover constantly looking for articles that may be of interest to my clients. When I see an item of interest to a particular client I send it to them with a handwritten note, 'Thought this may interest you…' they may have already seen it, but more often than not they won't have and will be impressed that you thought about them and took the time to add value for them, without wanting an order. The biggest mistake sales people make is contacting customers only when they want them to place an order. You can never hope to build a true relationship with this approach. By finding good reasons to keep in touch with clients you'll never have to ask for an order, because they'll ask you.

All of the above ideas will help you to build the networking bridge and put another link in the networking chain. Each time we make non-work related contact with another person our links grow stronger and stronger. We are constantly developing trust and earning respect. Networking is the glue that keeps relationships together.

So, when do the referrals start coming?

You will start to generate a regular stream of referrals as you build your profile. You will also find that when you start giving referrals away you will start receiving referrals. Let's look at some simple systems to ensure your flow of referrals is constant:

- Give away one referral every day. Become known for the number of referrals you give away and for helping to build other people's businesses (read more about 'revenue enhancement' as a networking strategy at the end of this chapter). Explain clearly to the person receiving the referral that you expect them to do their personal best for this person and that you expect them to get back to you and let you know how it goes. If these two criteria are not met, you may consider finding another person who values your referrals more. Feedback is critical so you know whether you are giving good referrals.

- If you refer business to someone whom you have met socially but have never done business with, mention this to the person requesting a referral. It is important to always protect your good name. Also ask this person to get back to you and let you know if the supplier met their expectations.

- You need to have a system in place to thank the person each time you receive a referral – whether email, fax, a phone call, a bunch of flowers, bottle of wine, magazine subscription and so on. I recently polled a group of 100 people about whether they would prefer a written or a verbal thank you for giving a referral. Ninety-seven people said they would prefer a written thank you. People pin written thank you notes on their notice boards, show them to other people and remember them. If 99 per cent of your business could come through referrals, would it be worth having a system in place to acknowledge these gifts? Yes – referrals are gifts, they were given to you freely.

- If you have no intention of using referrals, don't ask for them. Some people spend all their time collecting referrals and then never follow up. Wasting people's time is a real networking sin.

- Diarise time this week to track your last 25-250 clients – where they came from, the dollar value of past and potential business opportunities with them, and how much money was spent to get their business in the first place. If the business came from a referee or a sphere of influence, did you acknowledge or thank that person and advise them of the outcome of the lead?

- Create and maintain a database of prospects and aim to add to this list every week. Keep updating information about these potential clients until you have their complete contact details, including a list of their interests outside of work and any of their major achievements. The more you know about someone the easier it is to communicate and network with him or her regularly.

- The universal law of recency states that the person who made the last contact, more often than not, is the person who gets the business. Not everyone has effective data management systems in place. So when potential customers need a new supplier or want to re-connect with an old supplier, they often have no way of tracking where your business card is or how to connect with you. If you are regularly sending prospects and clients an e-zine, newsletter, update, new product release, or just a keep in touch article, you make it easy for people to do business with you.

- Spend money locally. Spending money in your community not only contributes to the local economy and provides employment opportunities, but it is a great way of showing support for others. Sometimes you might pay slightly more for certain products, however, if you want people to support your local business, look at how you can support theirs.

- Always ask the new client or prospect, 'How did you hear about my business?' If you don't ask the question you won't know which of your marketing strategies is working for you.

What you give away comes back tenfold. The law of reciprocity can give us a steady flow of leads and referrals. If you are unable to give a daily hot business lead, think about referring a restaurant, movie, a great supplier or a positive customer appreciation story within your network. As this becomes a daily habit, you will find that you start to receive daily referrals from others. The interesting phenomenon with referrals is that the people you give the referrals to are always indirectly connected to the people you receive referrals from. What goes around comes around. Mastering the art of giving referrals takes practice but when mastered, will ensure the growth and longevity of your business.

Networking Millennium Style: how you can make money by making money for your clients

Business today goes to those service providers who constantly exceed their clients' expectations and who grow their clients' businesses, as well as their own. In the US, it's called 'revenue enhancement' – basically it means making money for your clients as well as for yourself. This is non-traditional selling which has a powerful impact on your clients' bottom line, as well as your own. How do you do it and why would you bother?

The 'why' is very clear – client revenue enhancement enables you to stand out from your competitors and create far greater loyalty than you ever could through a price cut or special deal: in addition to your usual, exceptional service, you are giving referrals to your clients at no charge.

The 'how' is relatively easy and may just require a little lateral thinking on your part.

We know that the key to business growth is getting customers to buy twice, turning them into clients and ultimately, advocates. What if you graded your customer base into A, B and C category clients based on frequency or volume of orders (whatever criteria is meaningful to your business) to clarify exactly where the majority of your business is coming from (don't overlook the potential of small clients – you may be just one of a number of suppliers to them, if you are able to grow your share of their business, they may become a major client).

Next, look at each of these clients and ask:

- How well do I really understand their business?
- Do I have any idea of the type of customers they are looking to do business with?

The clearer you are on these points, the easier revenue enhancement becomes. If you realise that you don't know the answers to these questions, call your key contact within the client organisation and ask them to describe their perfect customer to you. Explain that as part of your client retention program you intend to refer business to them – and don't be surprised if they are taken aback with your offer. Also, ask your client to send you five of their business cards for you to give to potential prospects and make it easier for you to refer business to them. Create a portable referral business card folder (and electronic record of your client's details) and on the back of each business card, write your name – 'referred by John Jones'.

Once you have the information you need, ask:

- Do I know anyone who fits this description?
- Do I know anyone who knows anyone who fits this description?

You might not know anyone today, but you now know who you are looking for. Go through this process with perhaps ten clients at a time. Without doubt, you will find that you already know people, whether in your client base or among your associates, who are prospects for some of your clients. Now, it is simply case of connecting people.

Energy follows thought – what we think about in our lives is what we create. If our intention is to give referrals to our clients, we will find that this happens. It is as simple as having their business card available and giving it to prospects at an appropriate time. Linking people with similar interests and potential business opportunities is great fun and very satisfying. The by-product is often more business and referrals for you too – and all it took was a little of your time and a little lateral thinking.

Great networkers have an abundance mentality and truly believe there are plenty of opportunities for everyone. They are not afraid to do things differently and to help others as well as themselves.

chapter nine

planning your own networking events

neen james

Building Networks

If you can't find a networking group that seems to suit your particular needs, chances are there may be other people who share your frustrations – and there may be an opportunity for you to establish your own network.

Connect: Marketing Professionals Network, *www.connect.com.au*

Connect was co-founded in 2002 by Carolyn Stafford, Alison Hanlon and myself. We had each built our careers in the corporate world and were about to embark on our own business ventures. Our vision was to create a safe networking environment where like-minded marketing and communication professionals, operating as small businesses, could come together to share ideas, create alliances, cheer-on each other's wins – and to network.

We had a clear vision of who would be attracted to a group like Connect and knew that there was a real gap in the market. Very quickly word got out and there are now Connect chapters in both Sydney and Melbourne meeting every month. More than just a meeting forum, Connect features high profile guest speakers from around the world, enjoys the Patronage of Global Networking Specialist, Robyn Henderson and gives members the opportunity to give back to the global business community: a portion of every membership contribution is given to Opportunity International – an organisation helping people in third world countries to establish their own businesses.

Creating, growing and managing a networking group is a significant and ongoing commitment. From the beginning we were clear that Connect was about creating an opportunity for people like us to meet and grow their businesses, rather than a business that any of us wanted to make our own. We outsourced operations and invested significantly in a website that could handle all information, communications, memberships and event registrations.

Establishing your own network can take significant time and energy but it can also be very rewarding as you provide self- and professional development opportunities through exceptional speakers, watch people build relationships and alliances that they may never otherwise have been able to – and see the regulars coming back month after month.

These valuable strategies and lessons we learnt from creating Connect may help you if you're interested in establishing your own network:

Determine your focus. Ask yourself, "What is the purpose of this network?" Understand why you want to establish it and who should be involved. You may choose to specialise in an industry, like we did with Connect, or it might be a group for a specific segment, such as Women in Finance, www.wifnsw.com.au.

Set your strategy. Understand where you want the network to go, what it will achieve and how your members will benefit from being involved. It is helpful to get a few people to brainstorm ideas with and to contribute toward your strategic plan.

Decide the activity level. Regular activity is the secret of a good network. Choose a date once a month and always meet at that time, like the Last Thursday Club, www.writeanswers.com.au, which meets – you guessed it – on the last Thursday of every month. Connect meets in the same location for breakfasts on the first Friday of every month in both Sydney and Melbourne.

Decide functionality. A network requires a significant investment of your time so quickly establish a team of people to help you or a fully functional website to support you. Although the cost of establishing the Connect website was substantial it was money well invested and saved us time.

Get good support. Ask for a committee of volunteers to help you organise, run and follow up each event. You'll find a lot of people are willing to help and get involved if they believe in what you are doing.

Notes

chapter ten

ten ways to boost membership

robyn henderson

As networking becomes the norm in business today, more and more groups are emerging and competition for attendance can prove challenging. If you run your own networking group, or are invited to sit on the committee of a group, one of your biggest tasks will be to maintain and grow attendance.

Let's look at some practical, inexpensive and proven ways of boosting membership and making the R.O.A. (return on attendance) for participants more valuable, measurable and effective. Remember, more members = more networking opportunities for everyone.

Attendee nametags. Always, always, always provide nametags. Reports show that 80 per cent of people forget names within 30 seconds of hearing them for the first time. To help your attendees avoid this embarrassing situation provide nametags for everyone with their name typed in large (approximately 32-point), bold type.

Committee nametags. Most committee members are volunteers who give freely of their time. Providing a different nametag for committee members not only gives them recognition but also makes it easy for first-timers to know who to ask for more information and guidance.

Professional MCs. A great MC can make an event. Seeking out a professional from the ranks of your membership is an obvious solution, but just because Jack Smith has been MC-ing for ten years, doesn't necessarily mean he is right for the job; find a professional who is a good communicator, can keep to time, is non-sexist and has a commitment to the growth of the network. Many professional MCs will provide their services for no fee in exchange for the opportunity to gain exposure to your network.

Promptness. Reward members and guests who arrived on time by always starting and finishing on time. Starting late to accommodate latecomers only rewards negative behaviour.

Meeters and greeters. Their job is to 'meet and greet' guests with a smile and a self-introduction. Most of the fear associated with attending networks for the first time is specifically related to the first ten minutes. A 'meeter and greeter' takes the pain out of this process and can introduce first-timers and new members to others with common interests.

Ask me. Encourage some of your committee members to wear an 'Ask Me' badge. The MC will identify these people and their role is to mix and mingle throughout the event answering questions and providing information as needed.

List of attendees. Providing a list of attendees to everyone is a great way to facilitate networking during and after the event. Include people's name, company name and position with or without an email address; during the event people can highlight the names of people they meet. It's a good idea to draw attention to the fact that the information on the list is provided confidentially to attendees.

Business card corkboards. As an alternative to the attendee list, provide a double-sized corkboard on which people can pin their business cards as they arrive. Everyone will be able to see exactly who is in the room and the 'meeters and greeters' can help to connect people.

Membership application forms. Most networks want members, yet less than 50 per cent of networks actually have membership forms available at their meetings – it is such a simple thing, yet is often forgotten. Some networks encourage people to go to their website and join online which is fine, but why not have membership forms on hand to capture potential members while they're hot!

Testimonials. Why not invite one of your 'advocates' to do the membership spot for you. Asking enthusiastic, visible members, who attend regularly to say in two or three minutes what they have gained from membership is a powerful advertisement for the group as well as an opportunity to give members recognition.

chapter eleven

building relationships with sponsors & business partners

kim m^c^guinness

The Businesswomen's Breakfast Series, *www.centrumevents.com.au*

The Businesswomen's Breakfast Series is a not-for-profit networking event produced by Centrum Events. It was launched in March 1999 and holds monthly breakfasts at the Westin Sydney, Crowne Plaza Parramatta and Grand Hyatt Melbourne.

Its charter is to provide education, information and inspiration to the growing number of businesswomen in the greater Sydney and Melbourne areas. Each month, women from both the corporate and entrepreneurial worlds meet, exchange information and network over breakfast while hearing from speakers especially selected for their knowledge, advice and inspirational message for career women.

When the Breakfast Series began, there was a very limited number of networking opportunities available for career women interested in personal development and looking for a quality forum within which to expand their contact base. Its goal was to provide effective and valuable information alongside regular networking without the high membership fees charged by many organisations. Today, the Businesswomen's Breakfast Series has grown to become the largest regular networking event for women in Australia.

The high cost involved with producing events of this calibre requires sponsorship and funding; the Businesswomen's Breakfast Series would not have been able to survive without the support of sponsors.

What is networking event sponsorship?

The International Chamber of Commerce defines sponsorship as: 'Any commercial agreement by which a sponsor, for the mutual benefit of the sponsor and the sponsored party, contractually provides financing or other support in order to establish an association between the sponsor's image, brands or products and a sponsorship property in return for rights to promote this association and/or for the granting of certain agreed direct or indirect benefits'.

Sponsorship can be either paid (where funds are provided) or 'in-kind' (where goods or services are provided): for example, your venue may offer a reduced catering cost in return for promotion of their accommodation services during the event; a gift company may provide a door prize in return for a mention of their business; an employment agency may offer staff for the event in return for promotion. You need to identify what your requirements are in terms of both dollars and services to produce your event and seek sponsors who can provide these to you.

I have been fortunate to never have had the need to approach a company directly for sponsorship of the Businesswomen's Breakfast Series. All sponsors have come through contacts and referrals – another testament to the value of networking! So how do you make your network or event valuable and attractive to sponsors?

Be clear on your brand. The right sponsor can enhance your brand; conversely a poor match between the sponsor and event can harm your brand. Look for sponsors whose brands and values align with your own – and never compromise – it is better to struggle without a sponsor than to sell your soul by aligning with a sponsor whose brand message conflicts with yours. The integrity and standards you live by in your network should be reflected by your sponsor's brand, and you must believe in them as much as they believe in you.

Stick to your agenda. Be consistent in your product offering. Allowing your event or network to evolve in a logical way is fine, but don't jump all over the place with different themes and goals. This is confusing for a sponsor who has specific objectives.

Show strong growth. Sponsors want to know whether their association with you will bring them new customers and increase awareness of their brand. Being able to demonstrate steady growth of your network over time will be very attractive to a sponsor looking for an ongoing source of new customers.

Support your sponsors. Treat your sponsors with respect; they are a vital ingredient in your success. Give them the visibility they require and get to know their company, products and vision. Be aware of your sponsor's objectives and work to fulfil these with passion and integrity. Speak about them in a positive way at all times to all people – not only is it bad business to speak poorly about a sponsor, but who knows where your next sponsor will come from?!

Protect your sponsor's rights. Keep sponsors to a reasonable number; too many just increases clutter, confuses guests and decreases the value for sponsors. If you have promised your sponsor exclusive rights to a certain area of the event uphold this commitment vehemently and don't allow others to interfere.

Research pricing. Work out what it will cost to produce your event, or maintain your network, and how much you can bring in through ticket sales, membership fees and other sources. Then, check out current sponsorship trends and find out what people are paying before you come up with your final price – don't be greedy and ensure that you offer value and benefits over and above your competitors. Decide how your sponsorship structure will work. Will you have different levels of sponsorship? Will you have one major sponsor or a mix of industries with equal billing? Make sure that you include a corporate hospitality component to allow your sponsors to attend the event with important clients and staff.

Maintain contact. Keep in touch with your sponsors before, during and after events, for the entire duration of their sponsorship – and then some. Make them feel involved, valued, respected and important, because they are. Treat your sponsors well, make sure that their association with you is a win-win situation and their decision to renew the sponsorship agreement will be an easy one.

Sponsorship provides an opportunity for a valuable partnership. Treat your sponsors with respect and work to cultivate a positive, productive relationship. Even after sponsors change direction and move on, respect their decision and stay in touch. You never know where they will pop up again and what synergy there may be in the future between your organisations. Other potential sponsors will see how current sponsors are treated and will approach you when opportunities arise if they like what they see.

Notes

chapter twelve

Breakfast network checklist

robyn henderson

The most motivated people you will come across on any workday are those who have dragged themselves out of bed to attending a networking breakfast. But, be warned, their expectations are high! The more organised you are the more smoothly the event will run, and the more your guests will enjoy themselves. This of course will result in them thinking favourably about you and your organisation.

It helps to create a checklist for your specific events and refer to it with each function you hold. Use this outline to give you a head start.

Pre-Event Checklist

48 hours before the event:

☑ Confirm numbers with the venue, allowing for no-shows and late arrivals.

☑ Confirm what time you can have access to the venue and the name of the person who will be opening up, if it is not a large hotel with 24-hour staff. If you have any doubts that the person may not arrive, get their mobile phone number. Call them the day before and let them know you may ring…better to be sure than sorry.

☑ Confirm the availability of parking and what time the parking station opens.

24 hours before the event:

☑ Prepare any giveaways and handouts. If the venue has a secure locked area, deliver boxes in advance, clearly marked with the function date, time and location.

☑ Prepare the final agenda and send a copy to anyone connected with the event, including the venue organisers. Be very clear on the time of serving hot food, the clearing of plates, pouring of coffee, and so on.

☑ In your agenda, allow 'networking time' – time to chat to the people at your table. You may also consider appointing a 'table captain' at each table. If it is a client function, the captain would be a staff member. If it is an external event, you may select captains from your personal sphere of influence group. It is important to instruct them on your expectations – telling them to 'act like the host and not the guest', gives them authority to take on the perfect host role and encourage introductions and interactions around the table.

- ☑ Confirm details with the guest speaker/s and ask if they mind the tables being cleared or coffee being served during their presentation.

- ☑ Confirm with the MC the importance of keeping to time throughout the function. Also encourage them to give the guests an overview of what they can expect and what time the event will be finishing.

- ☑ Double check any equipment required by the speaker and also what time they expect to arrive at the venue. Having their mobile phone number is very reassuring.

- ☑ Prepare nametags with bold type – 20-point or larger. Many people need glasses and don't wear them – large, bold type saves them any embarrassment.

- ☑ Confirm with staff who are assisting with the event what time you expect them to arrive and what their duties will be. Give them your mobile number and obtain theirs – just in case.

- ☑ Work out what time you need to arrive at the venue to be stress free, organised and totally enjoying the event. Work out your travelling time to the venue, allowing for delays – and then add an extra 15 minutes.

- ☑ Prepare the clothes you plan to wear and have a 'Plan B' in case the weather changes. Put any paperwork or last minute items you will be taking with you at your front door together with your car keys. If you are travelling by taxi, book it now for your preferred departure time.

- ☑ Set your alarm clock, drop into bed and dream sweet dreams. You are organised and have left nothing to chance. You are bound to have a successful breakfast function.

chapter thirteen

internal networking

Neen James

While there are any number of different networking groups and events that you can attend, some of the best networking can occur within your own organisation. Boosting your profile internally by being involved in both professional and social events can substantially improve your opportunities when it comes time for promotion or appointment to special projects. Building strong relationships with key people throughout your organisation can help you to access information, gain support for initiatives, influence decision-makers and tap into other people's internal networks and spheres of influence. It is well worth investing time in. Try some of these networking activities to boost your organisational profile.

Professional Networking Activities

Hold a 'brown bag' seminar. Invite your colleagues to bring their lunch to a seminar. Identify a topic that you and your colleagues are interested in learning more about, it might be specifically work-related or something of general interest to most people such as health, fitness, work/life balance, financial planning and so on and invite someone to give a brief presentation. The presenter could be either internal or external to your organisation, the important thing is that he or she is an expert in the topic and able to deliver a quality presentation that people feel was worth giving up their lunch hour to attend. Set the agenda so that there is time for people to meet and chat when they arrive, allow 20 minutes for the presentation, ten minutes for questions and a few minutes at the end for conversations and mingling. You could hold these on a monthly basis and invite your colleagues to suggest topics for discussion. Make a point of taking the opportunity to meet someone from another department at each seminar.

Hold a quarterly breakfast forum and invite the CEO. Invite your CEO to attend a quarterly breakfast where he or she can meet with your the team and answer any questions they might have. Book the meeting dates in everyone's diary well in advance and make sure that people commit to attend. Ensure that you start and finish strictly on time so that the breakfast doesn't interfere with anyone's other commitments for the day.

Organise cross-functional team events. Invite another team to morning tea where team members can get to know each other and talk about what they do within the business and the challenges that they face. This is a great way to learn more about others and how different parts of the organisation work together, as well as to share information about the projects each team is working on.

Get in a project team. Seek out opportunities to work on projects both within your team and with other departments. This is a great way to demonstrate your abilities, to build relationships and to learn from others.

Offer to be the MC. If your organisation is having a conference or event, offer your services as the master (or mistress) of ceremonies. You'll not only have the opportunity to meet and work on the event with people from within your organisation, but also with any external consultants that might be involved in or invited to attend the event.

Write for the company newsletter. Offer to provide articles or updates for the internal newsletter. This is a great way to position yourself as someone who knows what's going on and to get your name in front of the whole organisation.

Provide your business card to co-workers. When you meet someone from another department always offer your business card. Particularly if you work in a very large or widely dispersed organisation, this will help them to know how to get in touch with you again.

Seek out (or start) a mentor program. When you invest your time in being a mentee you will be rewarded with accelerated learning and experiences from your mentor. You will learn from and avoid the mistakes that they may have made, learn about your industry, meet great people, form valuable relationships and be able to mentor someone in your future. If your organisation offers a mentoring program, sign up and get involved. If there isn't a formal mentoring program, suggest one or identify people you would like to learn from and approach them about mentoring you. If you are going to approach someone about being your mentor make sure you present yourself professionally and show your prospective mentor that you are serious and committed by having a mentoring plan in place (see box).

Guidelines for Effective Mentoring Relationships

Have a written agreement. Put your mentoring agreement in writing by outlining each person's responsibilities and commitments.

Set a time limit. Limit your formal mentoring relationship to six months. This gives you a timeframe within which to achieve your goals and learnings.

Meet monthly. Make a regular time (that is convenient for your mentor) for a one-hour meeting each month. Plan to meet in a location that suits your mentor, whether it is his or her office, favourite coffee shop or some other place they suggest.

Set an agenda for each meeting. Keep an ongoing list of things you would like to discuss with your mentor as issues arise throughout the month. Let your mentor know what you would like to discuss, what challenges you have been facing and what questions you have a few days in advance. If you can't meet in person, book a teleconference and run the meeting in the same way as you would if you were face-to-face.

Do your homework. Your mentor might give you activities to try or challenges for the next month – always complete these tasks and report back on your success.

Promote your mentor to others. Always take the opportunity to let others know about your mentor's skills, achievements and successes.

Thank your mentor with the gift of service. Being a good mentee is all about serving your mentor to create opportunities through which you can draw from their experience – offer to assist them with a project, help out in their business unit, drive them to an event or take them to the airport.

Do your homework on your mentor. Find out what your mentor likes to listen to, what books they read, which movies they enjoy and details about their family. This helps you to find areas of common ground where you can deepen your relationship and also thank them in ways that are important to them.

Maintain confidentiality. Keep discussions between you and your mentor private. Never disclose details of your discussions with others.

Avoid contacting your mentor outside of agreed times. If you agree to meet once a month, save your discussions for this meeting. If you do need to contact them outside of this time, use email so that you don't interrupt their daily activities.

Try to outdo your mentor. Learn from their experiences but always try and develop your own work that is even better than your mentor's. If you are successful, you could share your new ideas with them and add value by improving their business.

Social Networking Activities

Volunteer for the social committee. Every business has a social committee whether formal or informal. Invest some time in volunteering for the committee and helping to organise fun activities through which you and your co-workers can get to know one another. Plan for a variety of social events that give everyone the opportunity to get involved and to occasionally include their families.

Get involved in a charity. Identify a charity or good cause that people can get involved in supporting by participating in events, fundraising or donating goods or services to. Invite someone from the organisation you choose to support to update your colleagues on their activities and offer suggestions about how your organisation can help even more. This can be a fun way to help others while helping you get to know the people you work with.

Start a book club. Find people who are interested in similar books to you and start a book club. When you get together, talk about what you learnt from the book, your opinions on the writing style and what you liked most about it. If the author is local, invite him or her to join your meeting.

Start Friday night after work drinks. Suggest that your team finishes at 5pm on Friday afternoon and meet at a local bar or café. Invite other teams that you work with to join you. Make the 'official' time for drinks between 5pm and 6pm so that those who want to get away feel comfortable doing so. Choose a location close to the office and make it a regular event. After a month it will gain momentum, people will know that you'll be there and join you when they leave the office.

Organise a lunchtime sports team. This is a great way to build teamwork and get to know people from other areas within the organisation. Put up a notice or send an email asking for interested parties and form a basketball, football, tennis or soccer team or even a walking club. Meet at a nearby oval, park or gym at the same time each week. This is a great way to get some fresh air and exercise while networking.

chapter fourteen

aromatic networking:

creating an environment for success

jennifer jefferies

Picture this: you are at a networking event; there are 50 people in the room, including you. You are all there in the hope of expanding your business by meeting someone new or catching up with someone you've met before. You are all there to make an impression. How will you make yourself stand out in the minds and memories of everyone who meets you?

Have you ever noticed how your memories are locked-in to your sense of smell? We've all experienced the power of an aroma that instantly transports us to another place and time: like when you pass by a bakery and the smell of fresh bread baking instantly brings back memories and warm, fuzzy feelings from your childhood.

In the same way, you can use aromas to create a powerful point of difference, to set yourself and your business apart and lock-in the memory of meeting and working with you as a pleasant connection. I'm talking about more than just wearing your favourite perfume. I'm talking about tapping into and utilising the emotional properties of pure aromatherapy essential oils.

Unlocking confidence and creating memories

Most of the information published, and the work that aromatherapy practitioners do in clinics, focuses on the physiological effects and benefits of essential oils: in my clinic, I have primarily worked with their emotional and metaphysical benefits. These are less well known, but are by far the most powerful aspects of essential oils as they deal directly with creating positive memories and associations in a person's brain.

Essential oils affect the body and mind through our sense of smell and through interaction with our body's natural chemistry. When oils are inhaled, olfactory receptor cells are stimulated and the impulse is transmitted to the emotional centre of the brain: the limbic system. The limbic system connects areas of the brain linked to a number of body systems as well as to mood and memory. The properties of the individual oil, its fragrance and its effects determine how these systems are stimulated.

The use of essential oils in a networking environment is very practical and can draw on both the physiological and emotional properties of oils to create a positive environment and positive memory associations. This can be done on a large scale by vaporising oils which give people throughout the room a sense of ease and wellbeing, or on a smaller scale by creating a special aromatherapy perfume blend which you wear for your own benefit and the benefit of those close by you.

Imagine attending a networking event where you feel confident enough to introduce yourself to anyone in the room; where you are totally present and receptive to everything that you hear and where you are able to hold comfortable and balanced conversations that leave everyone feeling excited about the prospect of doing future business together. Using essential oils can't guarantee that you'll be successful with everyone you meet – but they can help you to draw on the courage and confidence you need to increase the number of quality connections you make at an event. If over-excitement and enthusiasm is more your issue, you can use grounding essential oils to help you maintain a calm confidence that doesn't railroad people and ruin chances for future business opportunities together.

Oils Ain't Oils

The first aroma most people think of when aromatherapy is mentioned is Lavender. That probably has something to do with the fact that most of us received Lavender soap from our grandparents years ago! Don't worry, you're not going to smell like your grandmother's Lavender soap when you create a blend to wear to your next networking event: we're going to focus on utilising some of the more dynamic essential oils.

So what are aromatherapy essential oils? Basically, essential oils are the fragrant elements that can be taken from just about any part of a plant: flowers, flowering tops, leaves, fruit, rinds, seeds, bark, roots, resin and berries. In some cases several different oils can be taken from one plant: the orange tree for example gives Neroli from the flowers; Petitgrain from the leaves; and Orange from the fruit. Each of these three essential oils has its own distinctive personality and therapeutic properties.

To receive the therapeutic benefits of essential oils, you must use genuine essential oils – not synthetic replications that are no more than perfumes or fragrant oils. Synthetic oils, even if chemically similar to pure essential oils, lack the natural elements that make pure oils so valuable for therapeutic use. To ensure that the essential oils you buy are 100 per cent pure make sure you check the packaging and labelling:

Packaging. Essential oils are always stored in amber, blue or green glass bottles; the coloured glass protects the oils from light.

Labelling. The label should include:

- ✦ Both the common name of the essential oil and the botanical name of the plant it originated from.
- ✦ The part of the plant used to manufacture the oil (different parts of the plant yield different types and quality of oils).
- ✦ The name of the country where the oil was produced (the same botanical species can produce essential oils with different chemical compostions when grown in different environmental conditions.)
- ✦ The ingredients, that is, whether the oil is 100 per cent pure or diluted with another oil such as Jojoba (pronounced ho-ho-ba); there is a big difference in price between 100 per cent pure essential oil and diluted oil. Some essentials are very expensive to produce because of the quantity of plant material required to extract the oil and the price should reflect this: for example, it takes approximately 30-40 roses to produce just one drop of rose essential oil, which is why pure rose oil is incredibly expensive!

- A TGA (Therapeutic Goods Administration) license number; this shows that the oil is registered with a government body and is guaranteed to be what it claims to be.

Aromatherapy Safety

There have been many claims made about the safety of essential oils over the years. You may be familiar with some of the warnings about certain oils. Much of this information, however, has been based on the internal use of herbs and not the essential oils. Research by London-based experts Robert Tisserand and Tony Balacs, who are considered world-leaders in essential oil science, has shown that the essential oils available over the counter in most retail stores are safe if they are used in the traditional ways of aromatherapy: that is through inhalation, massage and compress. Reports of adverse effects from using essential oils used in these ways are extremely rare and there are no essential oils contraindicated for pregnancy, high blood pressure or epilepsy if used in these ways.

The Steps to Aromatic Networking

As a professional speaker I am constantly at networking events and my work depends on me being able to differentiate myself from other speakers in the industry. I also need my audiences to remember me. I achieve this in one of three ways, depending on the environment I am invited in to and whether I am presenting at the event or not:

1. I apply my aromatherapy perfume. I work with two basic blends (see one of my personal recipes below).

2. If I am speaking I give an aromatherapy wand or scented business card to everyone in the room.

3. If I am using the room for longer than a keynote presentation I scent the whole room using an essential oil vaporiser.

Before the event

Your aromatic perfume

Using an aromatic perfume is the easiest (and my favourite) way to use essential oils for any meeting. It's easy to blend your own aromatherapy perfume: start with a bottle of pure Jojoba Oil. Any of the recipes in this chapter can be used to create an aromatherapy perfume – simply triple the number of drops of essential oil shown in the recipe and add to a 50ml bottle of Jojoba Oil. To apply, put a couple of drops on any pulse-point just like you would with any perfume. It's that simple.

This is one of my favourite blends that I wear to networking events. It is blended primarily to help me prepare myself, rather than to lock-in a memory for the people I meet and I find it works very well for me. Those around you will think that you simply enjoy wearing interesting perfumes; but you will know that you are receiving the emotional benefits of the fragrances as well.

Jojoba Oil		50ml
Vetiver	(grounded and centred, 'un-messable)'	3 drops
Bergamot	(cheers your heart to regain confidence)	12 drops
Basil	(speak and express yourself confidently)	5 drops
Rosewood	(be receptive to all that is possible)	10 drops

Essential oils on the road

If you have been invited to attend a networking event away from your workplace, you can still take steps to control your environment. Make your own Power Blend (see recipe below) to vaporise in your car on the way to the meeting. You'll arrive standing tall, feeling energised and self-assured – ready to take on the world feeling optimistic and focused, but also in an emotional space ready to listen and network.

Car diffusers, which plug into the cigarette lighter in your car, are available for vaporising oils on the move. This is a great way to prepare and get your head around the event while you're on your way there. The scent lasts up to a few days and you'll receive the emotional and physical therapeutic properties of the particular essential oils you choose.

At the event

So, you arrive having done the basics of applying your aromatic perfume and/or driving to the event in your aromatic car. You now want the people you meet to take away a lasting memory of you and what you do. The easiest way to achieve this is with aromatic business cards or wands.

Aromatic business cards

Choose three or four essential oils that suit the outcome you are seeking and blend drops of each oil in a small bottle. Put one drop of the blend onto each of your business cards. It might be that you want the people you are meeting to feel uplifted and optimistic – and therefore to be receptive to you and your message. In this case you could use a drop of a blend that contains Rosewood (be receptive to all that is possible), Grapefruit (be optimistic) and Orange (fun in a bottle – lighten up and stop being so serious). Any of the recipes in this chapter could be used to create your aromatic business cards, or you could create your own blend. You might even mention the fact that your cards are scented as you introduce yourself by saying: "Would you like one of my aromatic business cards?" Believe me, people love aromas. By using just one drop of your blend, the aroma will be subtle but powerful and not strong enough to be 'in their face' or to annoy them.

Aromatherapy wands

I use these at every event where I speak. It uses exactly the same system as scenting your business cards, but instead I use wooden tongue depressors ('wands'). I choose from a couple of blends depending on what I want to create. I then add one drop to one end of each wand. On the other end of the wand I place a small label printed with my details. So simple, but each person takes away an anchor and memory of me and my work.

Oil vaporisers

If you can, be in control of the environment. Set the atmosphere in advance so that the air within the meeting room greets the participants, putting them in the mood for constructive work. I prefer to use electric oil vaporisers in the workplace. They are safe, efficient and you don't have the worry of naked flames and water. Select the essential oils of your choice and add ten drops to the vaporiser, plug it in and turn it on. The ceramic bowl produces just enough heat to release the scent of the essential oil.

After the event

Keep the theme by sending a scented thank you card to those people you meet. Again, if you use only one drop, it will not overpower them or make them think that you're trying to be romantic! What you will be doing is creating a positive memory association and a powerful point of difference.

Aromatic Recipes for Successful Networking

These blends are suggestions for oil vaporisers. You may choose to create your own blends – 'tease your nose' and enjoy creating your own combinations that suit you and your organisation uniquely.

✦ ***Emotional Energizer***

Stimulate your mind and emotions to achieve all that is possible for the day; be ready to tackle anything that arises.

May Chang	*Stimulating*	3 drops
Mandarin	*Happiness*	4 drops
Rosewood	*Receptive*	3 drops

✦ ***Power Blend***

Draw on your stamina and reserves of inner strength to push through self-imposed barriers. Find your confidence and sense of self-worth recharged and your outlook to be positive, focused and optimistic.

Ginger	*Stamina*	2 drops
Grapefruit	*Optimism*	3 drops
Nutmeg	*Increases Energy*	2 drops
Pine	*Raise Self-Worth*	3 drops

✦ *Grounding*

This is for those who think too much. When you have a full mind to contend with, stay grounded and balanced so that you can achieve all you desire.

Vetiver	*Centred*	2 drops
Cedarwood	*Courage*	2 drops
Geranium	*Re-balance*	4 drops
Bergamot	*Regain Confidence*	2 drops

✦ *Improve Memory/Remember Names*

So important when networking. Stay stimulated and focussed. Expand your life experiences and allow yourself to use your mind and retrieve what is stored inside.

Petitgrain	*Retrieve Information*	3 drops
Lemon	*Rationality*	2 drops
Lemongrass	*Expansion*	1 drop
May Chang	*Stimulating*	3 drops

✦ *Relieve Overwhelmed Feelings*

Learn how to use oils to stay centred through times when you feel overwhelmed. Allow yourself to move between your conscious and subconscious mind to focus on the positives in the situation and to rationalise what is actually happening.

Petitgrain	*Retrieve Information*	5 drops
Lime	*Eases Stress*	2 drops
Vetiver	*Centred*	3 drops

✦ *The Perfectionist*

For those who think they are going to get it right every time. Better to have quality networks that work for you than quantity networks that go nowhere. Re-balance extremes, and be realistic. Release your attachments and ease the stresses that you create for yourself.

Geranium	*Re-balance*	5 drops
Clove	*Removes*Attachments*	2 drops
Lime	*Eases Stress*	3 drops

✦ *Releasing Negative Emotions*

Let go and live. Be optimistic about the future and focus on the positives. Nothing from your past has to influence your future unless you let it. See past negative patterns as learning experiences, and move on.

German Chamomile	*Let Go*	2 drops
Grapefruit	*Optimism*	6 drops
Cypress	*Transition*	2 drops

✦ *Fear of Success*

If you are living your dreams and not letting yourself get caught up in the past, you cannot fear the future. You remove and prevent any anxiety from creeping in because you have courage and feel supported in your goals. You will succeed. Get out there and do it.

Ylang Ylang	*Release frustration*	3 drops
Cedarwood	*Courage to make change*	2 drops
Bergamot	*Regain confidence*	2 drops
Jasmine	*Live with Passion*	3 drops

✦ ***Release your extrovert within***

Locate and release the extrovert within. Feel safe and confident to explore the possibility of freeing a passion that may have been hidden for some time.

Pine	*Raises Self Worth*	2 drops
Orange	*Lighten up and have fun*	4 drops
Rosemary	*Invoke confidence*	2 drops
Cinnamon	*Emotionally Warming*	2 drops

OILS	PHYSIOLOGICAL BENEFITS
Basil	Speak and express yourself confidently.
Bergamot	Cheers your heart to regain confidence.
Cinnamon	Release your extrovert w ithin.
Cedarwood	Be courageous and gain the strength to do anything.
Clary Sage	Gain clarity in w here you w ant to go.
Clove	Create possibilities by releasing attachment.
Cypress	Focus on moving forw ard through change.
Chamomile	Let go of negative patterns and habits.
Frankincense	Protect yourself from 'energy-suckers'.
Fennel	Assert yourself.
Grapefruit	Be optimistic.
Geranium	Balances perfectionist w orkaholics.
Ginger	Stop procrastinating and w arm your cold heart.
Jasmine	Live in the NOW w ith passion.
Juniper	Release negative thoughts and embrace change.
Lavender	Nurture your environment.
Lemon	Let go of irrational emotional outbursts.
Lemongrass	Remove self-imposed limitations and boundaries.
Lime	Ease through change and cruise through life.
Mandarin	Release your inner child.
Marjoram	Release unneeded anxiety.
May Chang	Rid yourself of 'poor me'. Jump in and be noticed.
Myrrh	Remove mundane thoughts. Release your dreams.
Neroli	Stop w aiting. Make choices now .
Nutmeg	Stimulate and revitalize emotional energy.
Orange	Fun in a bottle. Lighten up and stop being so serious.
Patchouli	Bring all areas of life together and enjoy balance.
Palmarosa	Embrace change and be adaptable to situations.
Pine	Increase self w orth and self-confidence.
Petitgrain	Retrieve stored information and ideas.
Peppermint	Find you purpose. Don't play others' games.
Rose	Nurtures your heart to regain passion for life.
Rosemary	Invoke confidence and creative energy.
Rosewood	Be receptive to all that is possible.
Sandalwood	Be still and peaceful on the inside. Contemplate.
Tea Tree	Release struggle and understand w hat is happening.
Thyme	Will pow er and strength to handle challenges.
Vetiver	Grounded and centred 'un-messable'.
Ylang Ylang	Release anger and be peaceful.

networking success stories

chapter fifteen

Networking your way to becoming 'wildly wealthy'

Sandy Forster

You've heard the saying 'it's not what you know, it's who you know', well I believe that it is actually 'not who you know, but who knows you'. Through effective networking and strategic alliances you have the power to make more money and achieve greater success (at far less cost) than you ever could through any other form of paid promotion or marketing.

They say your net worth is equal to your network, and I've experienced this first hand. Four years ago I owned a business designing, manufacturing and retailing surf wear. I worked seven days a week, had unreliable staff, huge overheads, never-ending problems and a growing debt. By the time I closed the doors I owed more than $100,000 and wondered how I would ever get ahead. When I started my new business I had nothing more than an idea – yet within five months I had generated close to $2,000,000 solely through strategic alliances. But networking hasn't always been easy for me...

Being somewhat introverted and a little anti-social (well, alright, a lot anti-social), networking used to be a word that terrified me; I looked forward to networking like I looked forward to having a tooth pulled! The idea of meeting and greeting, and making small talk with strangers in the hope of establishing a connection that would in some way prove beneficial was terrifying to me; I would have much preferred to be at home reading a good book or working on ideas for building my business…that was until I discovered the easy way to network and form strategic alliances.

What I discovered is that you don't have to be an expert in whatever business it is that you want to build, nor do you need to be a marketing expert (or even hire one) you just have to connect with the right people. Let me give you an example…

After years of money struggles I made the decision to transform my life. I decided I would immerse myself in learning how to create wealth and live a life of riches and abundance. I learnt so much about the subject of prosperity that I eventually trained to become a prosperity coach so that I could share what I had learnt with others. I built www.ProsperityCoaches.com into a successful business – I was making great money and having a whole lot of fun but I wanted to help far more people than I was reaching.

I came up with an idea – a mentoring program specifically for women. The idea was to teach women strategies to create a life of financial freedom. But there was a catch – while I was an expert on teaching mindset techniques and how to tap into long-forgotten secrets that can turn you into a 'Money Magnet', I wasn't big on the practical side of wealth creation – in fact, I found it quite boring. But as I said, you don't have to be the expert – just find someone who is. I teamed up with my accountant, Dymphna Boholt. She's a brilliant economist, accountant, taxation and asset protection specialist who knows the nuts and bolts of not only how to make money, but how to protect and keep it. Between my 'out there' metaphysical tips and her practical steps our business partnership was perfect; we call ourselves the yin and yang of wealth creation.

Together we brainstormed the idea of WildlyWealthyWomen.com and created a nine-month mentoring program that provided women with education, knowledge, support and strategies that could totally transform their lives. I built the website detailing how the program worked and we waited for the women to flock; and waited, and waited.

We knew WildlyWealthyWomen.com was a wonderful idea, but how would we tell women about it? I certainly didn't want to spend a lot of money; in fact, I didn't want to spend any money – mainly because I knew from the mindset techniques I taught that it was possible to just 'make it happen' through the power of thought combined with the right actions.

I knew in my heart that WildlyWealthyWomen.com was exactly what women were looking for, so I continued to picture it becoming a huge success.

Through a series of events I connected with an old friend, Rachael, who was finishing up a business in the travel industry. She was just starting her own company, which was based around helping others to achieve the same type of business success that she had. We told her what we wanted to achieve with WildlyWealthyWomen.com – that we wanted to get the word out to women all around Australia through television, radio, and in print, that we wanted to do it fast – and that our advertising budget was zero! Rachael agreed to become our marketing manager under a percentage of profits arrangement: if her marketing efforts paid off Rachael could earn a lot of money, if her marketing efforts failed, she would earn little.

Over the next few weeks, Rachael contacted television stations radio stations and newspapers all around the country telling them about our program and how we were searching for women so we could write a book about their successes. Many people in the media became as excited about the idea as we all were, and in the end, a number of newspaper articles were printed, including one on the front page of our local paper, and two television stations battled over who would win the right to run the exclusive story on WildlyWealthyWomen.com. We gave the go ahead to a national current affairs program and the story went to air a few weeks later. Within days we had received over 3000 hits on our website and hundreds of women from all around

Australia signed up for the program (it was after this experience that I decided I would never again pay for advertising).

It was a win/win for everyone: Rachael made far more money than she ever would have if she were being paid by the hour. And we were happy because hundreds of women were eager to be mentored about creating long-term wealth in their lives. Relying again on strategic alliances we have launched WildlyWealthyWomen.com in New Zealand receiving national media exposure in both print and on TV and we are planning to do exactly the same thing to launch in the US.

The power of networking has been demonstrated not only through our building the business, but also through the women in our WildlyWealthyWomen.com program. We have seen women from all around Australia creating miracles in their lives; women who have gone from having no money, no savings, no house, to owing three or more properties (all bringing in a positive weekly cash flow) in just over four months. We've seen single mums starting with not much to owning a number of properties and being able to quit their jobs to spend more time with their kids after just a few months. We've had a mother and daughter team buying ten properties with a positive cash flow of over $30,000 in three months. We've had women from all around Australia linking up to form joint ventures, to help each other find great deals, to support each other, nurture each other and network. It has been amazing and heart warming to see total strangers from all corners of our country form such a strong bond and network dedicated to helping each other create the future they have always dreamed about. The success stories of the women within our network are truly inspiring and it just shows what amazing things can happen when like-minded people get together with the aim of helping each other.

I love the idea of people being rewarded for helping me to grow my businesses, so I decided to launch an 'Affiliate Program' for WildlyWealthyWomen.com. Through this we make it possible for anyone who loves the idea of women helping women to transform their lives to spread the word and make great money at the same time (between $1000 and $1500 for every person who joins Wildly Wealthy Women.com). Women who have their own network, or a large database of clients, can potentially make tens, if not hundreds of thousands of dollars just by utilising their own network.

So as someone who used to hate the idea of networking, I have become a very strong advocate of what networking and strategic alliances can do for everyone involved. I have seen the power of networking and how it can help propel individuals toward success much faster than they could do on their own.

Do you think you could do the same? Do you think you could expand your current business, or business idea in a similar way? Of course you can. If you have a wonderful idea but not the knowledge, expertise or skills to make it happen – find someone who does. If you don't have the money to build your business, form strategic alliances with people who can make it happen with you, rather than for you. You don't have to be the expert to make money from an idea or business – you just have to know one!

One of the biggest tips I can give to anyone wanting to grow their business using virtually no money is to ask. I always say to my children – "If you don't ask, you don't get". Ask how you can help others, ask if others will help you, ask if they know anyone who could help you – just ask, ask, ask. The worst you will get is a 'no'. The best you will get is a connection with someone who is just the right person, or who knows the right person, with the ability to boost your business to enormous success.

The great thing is, when your success becomes known you will begin to have people coming to you to form strategic alliances and ask what they can do for you. This makes your networking so much easier and often you won't even have to leave home – I love the idea of that!

networking success stories

chapter sixteen

career networking

belinda yabsley

I come from a very humble background. I grew up in the northwest NSW town of Moree where my parents spent 50 years on the land as farmers and graziers. We were not wealthy in a financial sense but we were rich in values and love. I owe so much of who I have become and what I have achieved to the life-lessons my parents and family taught me.

My life today is a far cry from those days on the farm at Moree; I have been in the luxury motor vehicle industry for fourteen years, working for the past nine with international company DaimlerChrysler, selling new Mercedes-Benz vehicles from their factory-owned dealership in Zetland, NSW. I am currently the highest selling, highest profit-making and highest income-earning sales consultant in the Australian luxury motor vehicle industry. Last year I broke the long-standing record for the highest number of new

Mercedes-Benz' sold in a year and experienced a true career highlight this year with the sale of a One Million Dollar 'Maybach'- a vehicle hand built by DaimlerChrysler and considered around the world to be the pinnacle of motoring luxury. This was the first custom order ever taken in Australia for this prestigious motor vehicle, at a price of $1,000,000. More than the sale, my client, gave me the greatest compliment I could ever receive: "I have travelled across many countries in the world, met hundreds of salespeople along the way, yet you never gave up on me over the six years we have known one another. I have purchased 129 Mercedes-Benz in the last 19 years. I could have travelled to six different Mercedes-Benz dealers within ten minutes of where I live; yet I choose to deal with you. You are the reason why I am ordering the 'Maybach'. You are more interested in listening to what the customer wants than making the sale. Treat the customer like a King and they are yours for life".

Earlier this year, 90 per cent of my business came through repeats and referrals. Recently I decided to surrender my floor shifts in the dealership so other consultants could attend to walk-in enquiries - yet my business has continued to grow rapidly. Today, I maintain the position of number one sales rapidly. Today, I maintain the position of number one sales consultant with 100 per cent of my business now coming from repeat customers and through referrals.

I have always lived by the philosophy that 'my network is my net worth'. Treating people the way in which you want to be treated, giving without expectation, having a mentality of abundance, regularly giving away referrals, sharing ideas, information and cross-networking are the things I have done naturally throughout my life and career. Today we call it 'networking' - it is an essential life skill and business building tool, yet it is something that my parents taught me from a very young age.

My parents taught me:

To let people know they are appreciated. Caring for your customers does not have to cost a lot of money. It is about basic values and how you can make a real and positive difference in the life of another person. It's amazing what impact you can have simply by remembering a birthday or anniversary, celebrating the birth of a child, an engagement, a wedding, a promotion, a festive season or letting someone know that you care when they are unwell or in hospital.

To send a handwritten thank you note if someone does something for you or gives you something special. An interesting aspect of gratitude is that whatever you express, you will attract. When was the last time you received a handwritten thank you note? I send between 2500 and 3000 handwritten thank you notes every year. I say thank you for the business I do win and I even say thank you when I miss out on the sale, with something along the lines of, "Sorry I missed your business this time, however, I am always happy to assist you and your friends in the future" - this not only shows that you are a good sport but ensures that you are at the top of the list next time around.

That there is no virtue in acquiring something unless you are prepared to share the benefits and give pleasure to others.

Earlier this year I had the opportunity to share the benefits of my success in a way that I would never have imagined possible when I was able to buy my mother a new Mercedes-Benz for Christmas. Never in a million years did my mum ever dream of driving a new Mercedes! Words cannot describe the sheer delight and joy I felt when I saw her behind the wheel of her new car. And I know my late father would have a smile on his face right now, telling me, "You've not done too badly Binny; that's my girl."

Networking to Number One

I had no idea that I would end up in the automotive industry - when I left business college I took up a position as receptionist with York Motors, where I began my first networking database. I used cards to record the names of all our clients (along with their children's and pet's names), birthdays, work and home addresses, telephone and fax numbers, staff member's names, even the sports they played, their hobbies, any referrals they gave, the products they purchased, the details of their trade-in vehicle and any other special notes that would make it easier for me to re-connect with them the next time we met. Fourteen years later, many of the people from that card database are among my closest friends and clients who continue to refer enormous amounts of business to me.

After six months in reception I joined the service department as a service advisor. During the two years I spent in this position a number of customers wrote complimentary letters to my managers about how well they were being looked after and ultimately I was asked to join the New Car sales team. It wasn't long before I began to understand the difficulties of being in a minority (and a naïve one at that) in the man's world of selling luxury motor vehicles. This was a highly competitive, ego-driven environment. But rather than being scared off by this dynamic, or becoming part of it, I stuck with what I knew about working with people and focused more on my customers and their needs than I did on my end-of-month commission cheque. Within just two months I had moved into the number one position in the dealership specialising in new sales for Porsche, Audi and Volkswagen.

When Australians are asked what they think about car salespeople, most say that they do not trust them. I knew that I needed to break the mould, to raise the bar and pursue excellence. I knew that by listening to my customer's wants and needs and by making the experience of buying a car as memorable and pleasant as possible, my own reputation would be enhanced. As the Mercedes-Benz motto says, "Treat each customer as you wish to be treated yourself", if you do this part right, your customer will remain loyal to you and support you.

I treat my career as 'a business within a business'. People come into the dealership to buy a Mercedes-Benz, but many seek specifically to buy it from me - my name has become my 'brand'. What people want more than anything in any business is straight dealing and straight talking. People respond to honesty and reliability and my words are my legacy - If I say I am going to do something, I do it - my reputation and credibility are everything.

I give my customers a level of service that they will not easily find elsewhere. People come to me because they know I will listen to them and create a special, memorable and value-added experience for them. They know that they have found someone who will not only give them a straight deal, but more importantly, will look after them for a lifetime; in return, they usually refer everyone they know.

Building Real Relationships

The key is to keep in touch with your customers when they do not need your product or services - this is when you start to add-value and build a wall around your customer base against the influence of your competitors.

My clients know that no sale is ever final with me. My reputation is for keeping in contact and continuing to build relationships long after the sale. This might be through invitations to VIP events, tickets to the opera, to movie premieres, to exclusive wine tastings that I personally fund, and so on. I always find a way to keep in touch regularly with my network of customers and friends and am well known for remembering birthdays and anniversaries, for unique, unexpected presents and for courtesies such as picking up my client's Mercedes-Benz and dropping off a loan car when their vehicle is due for service. I also prefer to do business with those who do business with me and specialise in bringing networks and relationships closer where there can be a win-win for everyone.

Just as 'Mark Antony gave Cleopatra Cyprus and Richard Burton gave Elizabeth Taylor diamonds', I ask myself, "What interesting gifts have you given lately?" Gift giving is a buzz and finding the perfect gift for someone can be as much fun as receiving it. Why not visit Adrenalin Tours (www.adrenalin.com.au) and custom design an amazing experience for your client? If adrenalin sports are not to their taste, what could make someone feel more special than naming a real star in their honour? Your customer will never forget this gift, or you! Visit the International Star Registry (www.starregistry.com.au) to find something truly unique.

Selling luxury motor vehicles today is no longer a job - it is a profession and the people now applying for positions in the industry are quite different from the candidates of the past. Today we are seeing mathematicians, university professors and engineers applying - the only way to survive in this competitive world is to do what others are not doing - to be one step ahead of everyone else all of the time.

My most valuable asset is my relationships with my customers - without them, I have nothing and quite simply, if I don't look after my customers, and listen to their needs and wants, someone else will. By placing the customer at the centre of all my thinking, I have created lasting relationships and an environment of long-term success. It is called 'Customer Obsession' - it's about amazing service delivery, the realisation that no sale is ever final and reversing the pitiful service provided by so many retailers today. Customer obsessed businesses are rare but they provide a truly pleasurable experience for the customer.

Passion + Personality + Talents + History + Lifestyle + Wow Factor

= Profit

This, according to Walt Goodridge, author of 'The Tao of Wow' is the formula for success, "If you create and market a product or service through a business that is in alignment with your personality, capitalises on your history, incorporates your experiences, harnesses your talents, optimises your strengths, complements your weaknesses, honours your life's purpose and moves you towards the conquest of your own fears, there is absolutely no way that anyone in this universe can offer the same value that you do".

Indeed many years ago, I was told that if you find something that you love doing everything would flow from it, including money. Passion needs to be your main driving force; sadly, passion seems to be the missing link and the clue to what is wrong with retail today. Customers crave and reward memorable experiences.

Giving and Receiving Loyalty

Often I receive approaches to come and work for other manufacturers and for other industries, yet I feel a sense of loyalty to my customers, my dealership and to the Mercedes-Benz brand. Many people depend on me to provide information, sound and honest advice and to be responsive, reliable, empathetic, caring and flexible. I feel that I am no longer a product or service provider but have become a service partner - adding value, creating memorable experiences and always striving to exceed customer expectations. I am always on the lookout for additional ways that I can bring extra value and fun to the buying experience and continue to make my business one big customer service department - ever expanding, cross-selling and growing.

Networking Recommendations

I invest, contribute and regularly attend many networking breakfasts and seminars. What a brilliant way to start the working day - it is hard to believe that so many people can be so inspiring and full of energy at seven o'clock in the morning! Currently I am a member or participant in the following monthly networking groups, which I would recommend:

- Australian Business Women's Network,
  www.inspiringwomen.com.au

- Connect - for Marketing Professionals,
  www.connectnetwork.com.au

- Centrum Events - Business Women's Breakfast Series
  www.centrumevents.com.au

- New South Wales Motor Traders Association Women's Network

- Eastern Suburbs Women's Network (ESWN),
  www.eswn.com.au

- Business Network International (BNI), www.bni.com.au

- Women's Network Australia, www.womensnetwork.com.au

- Kids HelpLine 'Business Chicks' Breakfasts, www.businesschicks.com.au

- City SWAP (Sales People With a Purpose), www.swapaustralia.com.au

Networking for a Good Cause

The benefits of networking are not all about achieving business goals. After having spent the past 14 years building my network, I wanted to find a way to involve people, not only in a relationship in which we all had the opportunity to be of benefit to one another, but in a way that we could join forces and become united in helping to make the world a better place. I wanted to take the networking philosophies of abundance and win-win and channel them into helping a good cause in our community.

On 1 April 2004, National Smile Day was launched. Its objective was to raise close to half a million dollars for the Humour Foundation, an organisation which promotes the health benefits of humour and provides Clown Doctors to bring joy and laughter to sick children and their families in major children's hospitals throughout Australia (www.clowndoctors.com.au). The day was launched with a VIP cocktail function, which I was able to fill with 230 of my Mercedes-Benz clients as well as provide two celebrity MCs for from my network. Described by many of my customers as 'a night out at the Oscars', the evening also saw the launch of my new Mercedes-Benz customer award program. Twenty per cent of my commission from the sale of every Mercedes-Benz now goes to support the Clown Doctors. In return, my clients receive a special award to commemorate the donation, 'The Eternal Flame' (made by 'Lasercraft', an organisation which supports disabled people) - all that I ask is that they display their award proudly to help build awareness of this wonderful cause.

The ability to make use of my network in this way and to involve so many people in contributing to such a wonderful cause has been one of my proudest achievements and is an incredibly rewarding and satisfying position to be in today.

Without a doubt, the goldmine of opportunity will always lie within your humble database of past and current customers - and I always remind everyone I meet to never forget that 'your network is your net worth'.

Belinda receiving a 'cat scan' from Dr Peter Spitzer AKA 'Dr Fruit Loop'who co-founded and heads The Humour Foundation.

networking success stories

chapter seventeen

building a business through networking

neen james

I have spent most of my career as a corporate girl, having had the opportunity to work with some of Australia's leading organisations in the banking, oil, telecommunications and retail sectors. Through these companies I was able to study, completing my MBA, to meet fabulous people and to develop diverse skills. I became the General Manager of a telecommunications company, where I enjoyed all the trappings of corporate life – a top floor corner office with a view of Sydney Harbour, a personal assistant, a great team of people and an excellent infrastructure. But I wondered whether this was what I really wanted to achieve, and asked myself 'now that I am here, what's next?' It was then that I decided to leave the corporate world, to be brave, and to go out on my own. It has only been in the past few years that I have run my own small business, based out of my home.

The theme throughout my career was productivity. Today I am a productivity expert. By looking at how people spend their time and energy – and where they focus their attention – I help them to rocket-fuel their productivity and performance to achieve amazing things. I am a speaker, author and corporate trainer. I also like to be involved in multiple projects at any one time. I am a founding partner in the Cicero Project, www.ciceroproject.com, which helps people manage their message and become better presenters, and am also one of the co-founders of the Connect Network, www.connectnetwork.com.au, a small business network designed for marketing and creative professionals. But where I spend most of my time, is working with people to boost their productivity. I am fortunate to have some of Australia's biggest companies as my clients. All of my work comes through referrals and I believe that networking has been the key to my business success.

In the corporate environment many of the relationships you develop are formed by default through common projects and objectives. When you venture out on your own, you are solely responsible for generating your income and creating your work-life and you need to draw on the networks you have already established. It was my network that helped me when I set up my own business. I had to rely on the relationships I had built up over the years and to invest in new ones as people referred me to their contacts. I found that because I had invested so heavily in relationships throughout my corporate life and kept in touch with suppliers, management colleagues and even previous employers it was easy for me to get work once I announced that I was establishing my own business.

I believe that networking is the most powerful element in the marketing mix, yet it is not something they teach you at school or at university. Networking is not one of the '4 Ps of Marketing' but 'Personal Marketing' – networking, meeting people and developing relationships is the most powerful form of marketing. People do business with those they know, like and trust. If people like you they will do business with you. This applies both to clients and to strategic partnerships. By having great relationships with people, your working environment is more enjoyable and satisfying, you get to choose who you work with and your negotiations are always smoother.

Networking doesn't mean just meeting someone once and hoping they'll refer business to you. It is about staying in constant contact and building real relationships and it is vital to ensure that you remain 'top of mind' with your clients. By staying in contact with people, you and your brand are regularly in front of them and they will be more inclined to call upon you when they need someone with your capabilities.

One of my clients is a major Australian telecommunications company. It took eight months of having coffee every month with the decision maker before I had the opportunity to work with them – that was longest sales cycle I can ever remember, but it was really worthwhile. During those coffees I would learn about their business, find out about their challenges, keep up to date with their restructures and rarely did I talk about what I did – most of the time was spent learning about them. When the time came for me to work with them it was fantastic, I knew their acronyms, their decision makers and their protocols. They have now been an ongoing client for the past few years. This is an example of persistence too, when you meet someone you can't expect they are going to want to do business with you tomorrow. You need to earn the right to talk to them about what you do, which is what I did with this client. Now they ask me for so many different things that I have been able to introduce others to their organisation and help other people to grow their businesses.

I know that some people seem to be born networkers, while others struggle with it enormously! To improve your networking skills, practice the strategies from this book. Identify what you don't like about networking and how you plan to overcome those challenges. My best piece of advice would be to find someone who you think is a good networker, ask them to take you to a networking event and watch what they do. I did this recently for a friend who doesn't enjoy networking, she simply came everywhere with me during the evening and listened to the questions I asked, watched my body language, how I responded to people's questions and the follow up strategies I put in place for after the event. The next day we de-briefed the event to find out what her learnings were and how she could apply them the next time we attended an event. Often if you go to an event with someone, it doesn't seem so scary.

I belong to several networks and I do spend a lot of time networking. When I join a network the first question I ask myself is “What can I give back to this network?” – I think too often people ask the question “What can I get out of this network?” Approaching it from a perspective of giving means that I look for opportunities to help grow other people’s skills or businesses. And I believe that whatever you sow, you reap so much more. Recently I did two free workshops for one of the networks I belong to and a great result was watching two women (who had never met before) strike a deal and decide to do business with each other before the end of the evening. I know that work will result for me from these events but it is just as rewarding to watch other people benefiting too.

There are many benefits to be gained through networking. I love learning about what other people do, I like hearing about the progresses and challenges of different industries and I enjoy being surrounded by people. Networking broadens your skills and mindset. You meet new people who can stretch and challenge you and grow through being surrounded by interesting, intelligent people. I also benefit significantly as my business grows through word-of-mouth.

But by far the greatest benefit of networking for me is the opportunity to have exposure to amazing people who inspire me to become a better person and to continue developing and growing my business.

chapter eighteen

tools for effective networking

Networking Action Plan

Use this checklist to help you move you into the networking world quickly and effortlessly by thinking about your current and future networking needs.

Action plan - this month, this year

Monthly Action Plan

This week I need to purchase: (Tick as required)

Stationary

- ❒ Business Cards
- ❒ Business Card Holder
- ❒ - office
- ❒ - functions
- ❒ Thank You Cards
- ❒ Birthday Cards
- ❒ Sympathy Cards
- ❒ Everyday Cards
- ❒ With Compliments slips
- ❒ Letterheads
- ❒ Envelopes
- ❒ Blank Cards
- ❒ Diary

continued ...

Magazine subscriptions – Which industry magazines should I be reading?

Networking Functions

Which groups should I contact to ask to be put on the mailing list?

Which groups should I ask to remove my name from their mailing list?

Is my membership due for renewal?

continued ...

Which networking groups will I go to this month? (one per week recommended)

1.

2.

3.

4.

Have I registered and prepaid for these functions? Yes/No

Have I booked to attend any functions that I am now not available to attend? Yes/No

Who could I give this invitation to?

continued ...

Is there anyone I can invite to the functions I am attending?

Will I seek out sponsorship opportunities with a networking group this month? Yes/No

Yearly Action Plan

What companies would I like to do business with in the next year?

1.

2.

3.

continued ...

What past customers would I like to do business with this year?

What customers can I aim to turn into clients this year?

What clients can I aim to turn into advocates this year?

What can I do to get the ball rolling with the above clients?

continued ...

Do my website and stationery need a revamp? Yes/No

What image do I want to project for my company?

Are there any competitors that I could approach regarding some joint ventures in the next 12 months? Yes/No

Do I need to re-skill at all this year? Yes/No

If yes, what skills need my attention?

continued ...

Am I scheduling weekly fifteen-minute meetings with my staff to update them on the progress of the company? Yes/No

Do all of my staff have business cards? Are they using them?

How long since my staff re-ordered business cards?

What is my main goal or target for the coming year?

How can networking help me achieve this goal?

continued ...

Self Networking Tracker

Use this networking tracker template to help you to plan your networking activities and track your results. Make a copy for each month; at the beginning of the month complete section 1 – listing the networking activities that you have planned for the month – and at the end of the month complete sections 2 and 3 – reporting on what networking you actually did, what results you achieved and your networking plans for the next month.

Section 1: This Month's Networking Plans

Name: ____

How I plan to network for the month of: ________________

1. ____

2. ____

3. ____

Section 2: Review of This Month's Networking Plans

Key people I met:

1. ____

2. ____

3. ____

Value of business this month that I can track to past networking: $____________________

Section 3: Next Month's Networking Plans

How I plan to network for the month of: ________________

1. ____

2. ____

3. ____

Checklist for Making a Great Impression at Networking Events

☑ Remember your business cards. Have at least 25 cards with you at any one time. Keep additional cards in your car, briefcase, wallet, coat pocket or handbag.

☑ Carry blank cards in case you meet someone who doesn't have a business card with them. Ask them to give you their details on a blank card and offer them a couple of extras in case they meet others they want to give their details to.

☑ Always carry your diary. At networking functions you are often invited to other functions and could miss out on a great opportunity because you can't give a definite answer on the spot.

☑ Look out and befriend first-timers – those people who look a little uncomfortable and out of place. Remember every best friend was once a perfect stranger.

☑ Pre-book and pre-pay for the functions you plan to attend. If you can't attend on the day, try to send a replacement. Most organisers charge for no-shows.

- ☑ Turn off your mobile phone and pager during the function. There is nothing worse than listening to a great speaker be interrupted by a beep-beep. It is even worse when the person answers the call and starts having a loud conversation – there really is no faster way to turn the whole group against you.

- ☑ Decide prior to booking what you want to get from attending. If you just want a meal, go to a restaurant. Don't waste the time of serious networkers who are looking to grow their business.

- ☑ Read the daily paper or listen to the latest news on the day of the event. Select one or two topics that you will feel confident introducing into the conversation.

- ☑ Follow up if you say you will. Most people miss out on sales simply because they don't follow up.

- ☑ By the end of the function, if you are thinking it has been a perfect waste of time and you have not generated any business for yourself, find someone who you can give business to. With the law of reciprocity, what you give out is what you get back.

✦ thank you ✦

This book would not have been possible without the generous support of my co-authors – ***Belinda Yabsley, Neen James, Kim McGuinness, Jennifer Jefferies, Lee-Anne Carson, Sue Henry and Sandy Forster.*** I thank each of you for your patience, ability to stick to deadlines, make fast decisions and be as easy as you have been to work with – this has been a joyful strategic alliance and I feel very blessed to have created such a unique network of co-authors, with such powerful networking messages.

The book itself would not have been possible without a team of dedicated service providers including:

Simone Tregeagle – editor extraordinaire, who took our words and crafted them into a wonderful compilation of ideas, thoughts, systems and strategies.

Karen Curran – for designing our powerful book cover.

Toni Esser – our typesetter extraordinaire who made everything look that much better than we had anticipated.

Graham Wheatley from Watson Ferguson & Co. for his technical advice with the book.

Michael Franks for his legal advise on co-authoring.

Plus a big thank you to all the ***author's families, partners, friends, staff, clients and networks*** who have directly or indirectly influenced the content of each chapter. Thanks for all your support, encouragement and interest in our book.

And for ***you the reader***, we thank you for your purchase and we invite you to spread the networking word, either by sharing this book with others or as you improve your networking skills you too will become a light for those who are living in darkness.

✦ robyn henderson ✦

Global Networking Specialist, Robyn Henderson has authored and published ten books on networking, self promotion and self esteem building. She has spoken in eleven countries, presents over 150 times each year and has never advertised, all her work comes from networking, referrals and her website: www.networkingtowin.com.au

Her career includes over 12 years as a professional speaker, 10 years in sales and telemarketing management and 13 years in hospitality. Based on the far north coast of NSW, Robyn successfully launched Sea Change Publishing in 2004, to coincide with her recent move to the region. With a tagline – making the impossible, possible, Robyn believes everyone has at least one book in them and one of her goals is to show others how to write and self publish books on their passions and causes.

For more articles by Robyn or to make personal contact, visit:

✦ www.networkingtowin.com.au
✦ www.seachangepublishing.com.au
✦ Email: robyn@networkingtowin.com.au
✦ Phone: 02 66740211 ✦ Fax 02 66740233
✦ Mobile: 0407906501

✦ neen james ✦

Neen is a Productivity Expert: by looking at how they spend their time and energy – and where they focus their attention – Neen helps people to rocket-charge their productivity and performance. A dynamic speaker, author and corporate trainer, Neen demonstrates how boosting your productivity can help you achieve amazing things. With her unique voice, sense of fun and uncommon common-sense, Neen delivers a powerful lesson in productivity.

You can find out more at:

✦ www.neenjames.com

✦ sue henry ✦

Sue Henry has trained and inspired many small business owners to excel beyond their own expectations. Gifted with being able to immediately assess what a business needs to do to move it forward Sue's unique approach to sales, networking and innovative methods to building business is what sets her apart.

Sue is an avid consumer of business literature and motivational text, as a result her acceleration strategies, enthusiasm and passion for what she does and her ability to quickly assimilate new information make a powerful force for small business owners to learn and benefit from.

Sue is also known to enjoy a good laugh and round of golf!

✦ Small Business Accelerator,
Suite 203, 184 Blues Point Rd, McMahons Point NSW 2060
✦ Phone: +612 9420 3737 ✦ Fax: +612 9420 3737
✦ Email: sue@smallbusinessaccelerator.com
✦ Website: www.smallbusinessaccelerator.com

✦ sandy forster ✦

Sandy Forster has a passion for personal development, is a Certified Prosperity Coach, an author, speaker, entrepreneur, as well as raising 2 beautiful children.

She lives on the beautiful Sunshine Coast, is a life-long learner and loves reading and studying anything to do with the metaphysical, prosperity and personal empowerment.

She has a passion for helping others around the world to create a life filled with abundance and prosperity and is committed to sharing her knowledge while having as much FUN as possible!

✦ Wildly Wealthy Pty Ltd,
P.O. Box 362, Mooloolaba. Qld 4557
✦ Phone:1300-133-249
✦ Website: www.WildlyWealthy.com
www.MillionaireMoneyGame.com
www.WildlyWealthyWomen.com
www.ProsperityCoaches.com

✦ jennifer jefferies ND ✦

Jennifer Jefferies, "Life Balancing Specialist" is an accomplished author, international business educator, naturopath and aromatherapist. Jennifer is known for her dynamic, information filled presentations.

Her background includes over 14 years as an international professional speaker, and for the last 22 years she has owned or managed retail stores and clinics in Australia.

Jennifer's passion in life is informing people on ways they can integrate natural therapies into their work and personal lives to achieve the feeling that they are really LIVING and not just EXISTING.

- Living Energy
  PO Box 4298, Elanora, Qld 4221
- Phone: (07) 55986 035 ✦ Fax: (07) 55986 036
- Mobile: 0412 236 812
- Email: jennifer@livingenergy.com.au
- Website: www.livingenergy.com.au

✦ kim mcguinness ✦

In 1999, after a varied career in events, marketing and accountancy, Kim McGuinness launched her own events company, Centrum Events Pty Ltd. She has organised countless events from 10 to 2000 delegates but is most recognised as founder of The Businesswomen's Breakfast Series which began in July 2000.

Kim launched Network Central in September 2004, catering to the challenge of networking and support in each area of our busy lives. Kim, who herself has two young children, is studying and also running a business, understands only too well the demands on our time in an average day. Effective networking and a good support network in each area can be the key to success!

✦ Centrum Events Pty Ltd,
PO Box 334, Pymble Business Centre NSW 2073
✦ Phone: +612 9983 9406 ✦ Fax: +612 9983 1697
✦ Email: info@centrumevents.com.au
✦ Website: www.centrumevents.com.au

✦ lee-anne carson✦

A compelling professional, Lee-Anne is uniquely equipped with senior manager expertise proven by results in some of Australia's largest organisations across a broad spectrum of industries.

Lee-Anne has demonstrated over and over in such companies as Telstra, GE and News Limited how to take long term underperforming teams and build high performance individuals and teams within twelve months. All of this with a keen eye on both the internal and the external customers through successfully building and sustaining customer trust and loyalty.

A background in Social Work and post graduate studies in Facilitation, Performance Management, DISC, PERT, various Sales programs and Certificate 4 Workplace Training tops off over 25+ years of individual, team, group and corporate training. A passion for individuals, Lee-Anne engages and supports people constructively so that they are able to perform at exceptional levels.

✦ Performance Solutions International
✦ Phone:(02) 99744975 ✦ Fax: (02) 9974 1539
✦ Email: leeanne@performsolutions.com.au
✦ Website: www.performsolutions.com.au

✦ belinda yabsley ✦

At 30 years of age, Belinda Yabsley is "still a country girl at heart, forever achieving extraordinary things" in her amazing professional, personal, sporting and philanthropic life.

Belinda has been in the Luxury Motor Vehicle Industry for fourteen years and is currently the most successful new vehicle sales consultant in Australia. She is known for running her own business within the international organisation of DaimlerChrysler, specialising in selling new Mercedes-Benz vehicles. She operates from the factory-owned dealership in Zetland, New South Wales, notably the largest (most successful) Mercedes-Benz dealership in the country.

She currently holds 2 national records and has set amazing benchmarks for luxury motor vehicle sales, predominantly in a male domain and amongst the efforts of her large and competitive peer group. Belinda has built her client database from scratch to just over 3000 loyal customers and friends today with 100% of her sales now coming from repeat and referral business.

✦ C/o Mercedes-Benz of Sydney,
PO Box 883, Rosebery NSW 1445
✦ Phone:(02) 9697 7735 ✦ Fax: (02) 9313 7322
✦ Mobile: 0418 522 228
✦ Email: mbsales@belindayabsley.com
✦ Website: www.belindayabsley.com

✦ recommended products ✦

Products available at www.networkingtowin.com.au

This book will give countless invaluable tips on how to be see, get known and move ahead. We show you ways of building your profile that are so simple, so easy and so enjoyable, you'll wonder why you never used them before. **$27.50 inc gst**

If you want to have more time to network effectively and get a serious return on your investment, this one hour informative CD is a must for YOU! Pack contains a 60 minute presentation - interview style - with Robyn Henderson and Lorraine Pirihi. Also includes 2 bonus e-books! **$49.50 inc gst**

This practical 144page book will give you 366 instantly useful tips - one for everyday of the year. Advice which is affordable, effective and easy to implement. Generate endless referrals immediately. **$27.50 inc gst**

✦ recommended products ✦

This survival guide for shy or nervous networkers will arm you with effective conversation starters to enable you to talk to anyone, anywhere at anytime. Plus show you how to become a sphere of influence in your career and social networks and increase your return on investment from attending networking events. **$25 inc gst**

Everything you wanted to know about attending networking functions and strategic alliances and didn't know who to ask. In this easy listening interview style format, Robyn shares all her personal networking habits for you to implement and include in your busy life. With over 2 hours of content, this CD will give you simple yet powerful strategies to double your customer base today. **$66 inc gst**

This CD pack and workbook is full of "how to" tips including: adjusting to working in a home-based office, setting up your office environment, educating those around you, establishing systems and support for your business, planning and scheduling your days for maximum productivity, controlling the paper war, eliminating distractions, handling interruptions every day, and a whole heap more **$99 inc gst**

✦ recommended products ✦

Aromatherapy Networking Pack

This pack includes an **electric oil vapouriser** and 3 essential oil blends:

The electric oil vaporisers are workplace safe and cost less than 2cents a day to operate.

Mind Power: a mentally stimulating blend of lemon, peppermint, basil, black pepper and rosemary essential oils which help you stay focused and clear headed.

Sensation: an invigorating blend of grapefruit, may chang, black pepper, ginger and palmarosa essential oils which will energise and refresh your mind.

Grounding: nurture your soul with this earthly blend of australian sandalwood, vetiver, cedarwood, rosewood, patchouli and tangerine essential oils. A grounding blend designed to assist with adrenal exhaustion and help you stay balanced.

$99 inc gst

✦ order form ✦

To order any of these products or additional copies of this book please contact

- ✦ Robyn Henderson, Sea Change Publishing, PO Box 1596 Kingscliff NSW 2487
- ✦ Phone 02 66740211 ✦ Fax 02 66740233
- ✦ Email: robyn@seachangepublishing.com.au ✦Website: www.seachangepublishing.com.au

Or complete the following order form:

Title	Quanity	Cost per item	Total
Books			
Network or Perish		$25.00	
How to Master Networking		$25.00	
Be Seen, Get Known, Move Ahead		$27.50	
Networking Magic		$27.50	
CDs			
How to Double your Customer Base		$66.00	
Home Based Business		$99.00	
Get Connected		$49.50	
Packs			
Aromatherapy Networking Pack		$99.00	
MASTER PACK			
includes one of everything above		**$385.00**	
Postage & Handling (per order)		$15.00	
All prices include gst		**Total**	$

Name____

Address______________________________________

Phone________________Email________________________

❑ Bankcard ❑ Visa ❑ Mastercard

Name on Credit Card________________________________

Signature______________________Expiry Date____________________

Credit card number: ________________________________

or I enclose cheque for $__________ (please make cheques payable to seachange publishing)

✦ about seachange publishing ✦

Robyn Henderson, entrepreneur and innovator, founded Sea Change Publishing in 2004. As a Global Networking Specialist, Robyn had built a successful career throughout 10 countries speaking and writing about her passion - networking. At the same time, Robyn had successfully self-published six of her seven books on business networking, self promotion and self esteem building, as well as creating a successful e-business.

Travelling the world, Robyn met many interesting people and encouraged all of them to share their stories either through books, articles, ebooks or film. She realised that just the thought of writing a book overwhelmed many of these fascinating people - yet she knew their stories had to be told.

And as Robyn prides herself on being a solution provider for her many clients, she started running her popular 3 ways to write non-fiction book workshops throughout Australia and New Zealand.

These workshops were quickly followed by a CD series, telecoaching, one on one coaching, brainstorming and creativity clusters, writers retreats and a total project management of books from concept to completion. Realising there was major interest in all of these areas, Sea Change Publishing was launched. In 2003 Robyn experienced her own sea change when she relocated her business from Sydney to the far north coast of New South Wales, close to the Queensland border. Hence the name was a natural progression. And the by line - making the impossible, possible - is giving people courage to do what they see to be impossible.

Using her master networking skills, Robyn has been able to bring together a stable of experts to assist with every facet of book production: Ghost writers, editors, typesetters, graphic designers, literary stylists, proofreaders, printers, book marketing experts, public relations consultants and event managers.

Plus she has launched a book writing graduates network, which provides support and encouragement to fellow authors.

She has also formed a dream team of innovative thinkers, who are available to brainstorm ideas on book concepts, content viability, target markets and potential global markets for budding authors - unsure of the writing potential.

Robyn encourages her workshop graduates to think "series" rather than just one book. Often authors think they have to put everything they know into one book. This sometimes results in a book with a little bit about a lot of things rather than focussing on one or two areas and covering them well. She encourages authors to consider writing more than one book and once the original book is written to then write books for niche areas e.g. a book on leadership could be niched to leadership for bankers, leadership for real estate principals, small business owners etc. .

CRACKING THE BOOK DISTRIBUTION CODE:

Robyn has also set up a number of alternative book distribution streams other than the traditional bookshops. She believes, not only will this reduce the retail cost of books, but will also give self published authors greater access to the marketplace, not to mention giving readers a wider choice of material.

Robyn firmly believes that Sea Change Publishing will bring together all the skills that Robyn has learned over the past 50 years. She truly believes in making the impossible, possible.

For information about SEA CHANGE PUBLISHING, please visit

www.seachangepublishing.com.au

or email:

robyn@seachangepublishing.com.au

✦ index ✦

C